Praise for "Gymnastics: Boys Level 1 Coaches Certification Manual"

"I have been waiting for a boy's manual like this for some time. It's a great tool for the up and coming new gymnastics coach as well as the experienced coach. Good skills, good illustrations and I am excited that my staff now have an excellent reference book for the boys recreational program with great teaching progressions."

Wayne Kerr – USA National and International Coach

"Resumes give the club owners and managers backgrounds of their potential applicants. Many resumes don't give enough information about their gymnastics background and qualifications in the sport. Those who are GYMCERT Certified give the applicant a better advantage for the job. I always look to see each applicant's level of education and if they are GYMCERT Certified."

Al Fong
USA National Coach, Great American Gymnastics Express

"Instructor turnover at the recreational level of gymnastics has been an ongoing problem for most gymnastics school programs and hard to deal with, especially the training of our new recruits. The GYMCERT manuals and web based training program will save me a lot of time in presenting the basics of this sport. Certification of my instructors is also a great marketing tool for my program."

Tim Rand
USA National Coach, American Twisters

"It's about time there is an Educational Training Program for the grass roots of gymnastics. GYMCERT is the answer and a 10.00! Thank you, Gymcert writers."

Mike Jacki
USAIGC President, Former USA Gymnastics President

"Way to go, GYMCERT! It is a easy as 1-2-3. One, the text in the manual gives solid training training materials for the novice coach and the manual describes each skill. Two, each skill is fully illustrated in the manual with excellent technique!. And, three, my instructors can go online and see active video of each skill being performed along with coaching, teaching and safety tips!"

Vladimir Artemov
1988 Olympic Champion, Former Russian and USA National Team Coach

"Teaching Gymnastics is my passion, so along with GYMCERT's Boy's Instructors manual I am able to offer the best safety minded skills program form my entire boys' classes!" Thanks for making this a reality .I am proud to say my staff is now all GYMCERT Certified!

Kelly Donyes
Founder of GymAgine, Seattle Washington

Dedication

To Kelly Donyes and Wayne Kerr:

Thank you for your ongoing inspiration and encouragement to complete this wonderful project for the Boys Program. With out your ongoing support and critiquing I may not have been able to complete the first GYMCERT's Boys Gymnastics Coaches Certification Manual.

Acknowledgement

This book would never have been published without the guidance, direction, and writing/editing skills of Kelly Donyes. He is truly one of Seattle's Best!

Gymnastics: Boys Level 1 Coaches Certification

By Rita Brown

RJC PUBLISHING
Orlando, Florida

"Gymnastics: Boys Level 1 Coaches Certification Manual"
by Rita Brown (assisted by Gymcert Advisory Board Members)

RJC Publishing   **ISBN: 0-9745492-7-4**
740 Orange Ave.   **PCN: 2003098865**
Altamonte Springs, FL 32714   **SAN: 255-6189**

Publisher's Cataloging-in-Publication
(Provided by Quality Books, Inc.)

Brown, Rita.
    Gymnastics. Boys Level 1, Coaches certification manual /
by Rita Brown.
    p. cm.
    At head of title: USACERT.
    Includes bibliographical references.
    ISBN 0-9745492-0-7

    1. Gymnastics--Coaching--United States.
    2. Gymnastics coaches--Certification--United States.
    I. Title. II. Title: USACERT.
    III. Title: Coaches certification manual.

GV461.7.B76 2004   **796.44**
                            QBI03-200928

DISCLAIMER
This book is written and intended to be used as a guide only. The publisher and authors are not engaged in the profession of rendering any form of legal, technical, or medical advice. If for any reason legal, technical or medical advice is necessary, you should seek out qualified professionals.

The purpose of this book is to educate and acquaint individuals with basic safety concepts used in the sport of gymnastics. Every effort has been made to provide complete and accurate information on this subject. Readers of this book are strongly advised to obtain Safety Certification or Risk Management Certifications through the USAG (USA Gymnastics) as well as Certification in GYMCERTS Safety Basics.

The authors and USACC shall have neither liability nor responsibility to any person or entity with respect to any loss or damage caused or alleged to be caused directly or indirectly by the information contained in this book.

Illustrations: Wally Eyman, Rita Brown   Photographs: Heather Maynez, Rita Brown
Cover: Kurt Merkel   Cover Photographs: Rita Brown

Internet Access: **http://www.gymcert.com**

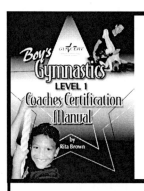

Gymnastics Certification Program
a subsidiary of USACERT

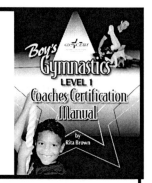

Contents

Special Notice:

It is an unfortunate sign of our times when the opening to a book must be a warning, however, due to the nature of this manual and the skills presented it is imperative that the gymnastics instructor understand the gravity of the situation.

Any activity in life from taking a bath, to playing baseball, even to having fun on the playground all carry varying degrees of risk for potential injury. A fall from the Jungle Gym, being hit with a bat or ball, or a slip and fall getting out of the bathtub may cause serious injury. In gymnastics, there is also the potential for significant injury, especially so when an instructor is not qualified through lack of knowledge or experience. Basically, the instructor must have the ability to adapt gymnastics technique to the size, weight, and fitness level of each gymnast; provide adequate supervision for the activity; be capable of spotting the skill; supply appropriate lesson plans using effective skill progressions and keep adequate records; and, be able to adequately warn each gymnast of the dangers inherent in each of the skills they attempt, while developing in the gymnast a motivated, positive outlook on skill acquisition.

The key to success for the gymnastics instructor is patience, a desire to learn, and mentoring from another more accomplished coach. Your desire to learn is obvious by the fact that you are reading this book to learn new training techniques and skill progressions. You should be aware, however, that the skills presented are based on one "average" (in size, shape, and fitness level) gymnast illustrated in each section. While the techniques presented may work adequately for this fictitious gymnast, they may not work as well for the slightly overweight and less physically fit gymnast. You, the instructor, will have to adapt the technique to fit the gymnast.

That being the case, the author and publisher of this book must warn you that responsibility for the use and/or adaptation of these techniques are the sole responsibility of the instructor employing them to teach a skill. The materials contained in this manual are to be used to provide a base level of knowledge about gymnastics skills and training techniques. It is strongly suggested that you seek advanced coaches within your program to mentor you and guide you in developing gymnastics technique, spotting skills, and training methods. When in doubt, always check it out with your mentor first.

Foreword

As a gymnastics club owner and consultant for several years, I have encountered the same frustrations that most Club Owners and Program Directors experience. Frustrations that increased in magnitude as I expanded my business and opened new gymnastics training facilities in other regions of the United States. The biggest issue I faced was the ability to find quality gymnastics teachers and coaches that had a background in gymnastics and experience teaching or training children. Applicants for the position of instructor were mostly young people who enjoyed, admired, or loved the sport of gymnastics. Some were past members of a high school, private club, or YMCA Program. In most cases, the applicants did not have any experience teaching gymnastics let alone any formal teaching certification or educational background; qualified instructors were just not available.

Hiring a Physical Education teacher who received a degree in either the Elementary or Secondary Education field was the only way to find a qualified instructor. At least these individuals had the background to access, organize, prepare lesson plans, and track their student's progress.

As an "expert" witness in lawsuits involving gymnastics cases, one of the first questions I am asked by an attorney is, *"How do you become a gymnastics teacher and what qualifies you to be one?"* In many gymnastics programs, the most qualified staff is hired to teach the competitive team members. The least experienced coach is setting the gymnastics skills foundation with the new students and possibly the future members of the competitive team. Because of this inequality in teaching ability, I realized there was a need to develop a series of reference manuals for the recreational class instructor starting at the beginner level and progressing through intermediate and advanced recreational instruction.

"Gymnastics: Level 1 Coaches Certification Manual" is the first of many such manuals. It is accompanied by GYMCERT's online training program that includes streaming videos and auditory explanations of each skill illustrated within the manual. Certification for the Level 1 program is also available at www.gymcert.com . The Level 1 manual references the basic introductory terminology and skills for the Level 1 gymnastics instructor. My goal is to help raise the standard of teaching through knowledge and real time feedback for the instructor, resulting in better gymnastics training for the beginner gymnast, which will lay the foundation for success at the higher levels of gymnastics instruction.

I believe that certification will produce the following favorable outcomes:

1. It will provide a better and safer environment for gymnastics participants.
2. It will raise the standard of knowledge for gymnastics coaches.
3. It will provide a system of accountability for gymnastics coaches and gyms.
4. It will help lower the risk for insurance companies, which could lead to lowering the liability insurance rates for gym owners.
5. It will provide club owners a method for determining the qualification of future employees and save them money through onsite training versus travel to seminars.

Enjoy your quest and journey into the wonderful sport of gymnastics! As several wise old gymnasts and coaches can confirm; once you have a taste, gymnastics is forever in your blood.

Rita Brown

Vladimir Artemov
1988 Olympic All-Around Champion

SECTION 1

Introduction

Welcome to coaching men's gymnastics. This program demonstrates the "excitement" of teaching beginning gymnastics in a "positive" learning atmosphere with the main emphasis on SAFETY and FUN! The purpose of this course is to create a base level of safety, planning, and motivational training that enables you to develop and become a more valuable instructor and effective teacher.

Gymnastics is an exciting and rewarding sport but it carries with it some inherent risk when performing, spotting, or instructing. No matter how well you plan your class there will still be the possibility, albeit greatly reduced because of your training, of a gymnast being injured. The key to reducing injuries and making your classes safe is prevention. To prevent accidents and reduce risk the instructor must constantly ask himself the following questions when planning and teaching:

1. Is the equipment properly set up, and is the surrounding area prepared for the performance of gymnastics skills?

2. Is the gymnast mentally and physically ready, and does the gymnast understand exactly what is expected of him or his in the performance of the skill?

3. Has the coach properly prepared himself or himself to teach the skill by using proper progressions, lesson plans, and learning the correct spotting techniques? (Feeney, p.27)[1]

4. Are we having fun yet?

And finally, the question which ties them all together: What's important now? You can remember this question by the acronym W.I.N. When you are stretching the class during warm up, ask yourself; what's important now? Look around your class; it might be helping a gymnast to focus on tight knees or possibly introducing a fun game to get the blood flowing before stretching. The key in each planned portion of your class is to look around, and in relation to the four questions above, always ask yourself, what's important now?

Certification

This course is geared toward new and experienced instructors that wish to pass the first level of boy's gymnastics certification. Passing this accreditation course will certify you to coach gymnastics at the Boys Level 1 or the equivalent of a Beginner level class. Before taking your own students or class you should practice your spotting skills and shadow your mentor or team level coach for as long as they feel

---

[1] Feeney, Rik. <u>Gymnastics: A Guide for Parents and Athletes</u>. Indianapolis: Masters Press, 1992.

you should. That experience is needed to become a proficient and confident spotter. Never attempt to spot a gymnast without having sufficient practice at spotting the skill. GYMCERT recommends that you become a member of USA Gymnastics at the Instructor Level or Professional Level and complete their USAG Safety Course/Risk Management Course. GYMCERT's Boys & Girls books including Level 2, Level 3, and "Safety Basics" courses are also available through GYMCERT online at www.gymcert.com

The Level 1 course is divided into 15 Chapters

SEGMENTS

Section 1: Introduction

Section 2: Legal Responsibilities…

Section 3: Basic Gymnastics Techniques

Section 4: Safety in a Gymnastics Program

Section 5: Spotting

Section 6: Conditioning: Strength & Flexibility

Section 7: Body Positions *

Section 8: Floor Exercise and Tumbling Skills *

Section 9: Vault *

Section 10: Bars *

Section 11: Pommel Horse or Mushroom *

Section 12: Rings *

Section 13: Parallel Bars*

Section 14: Trampoline   *

Section 15: Conditioning Exercises for Level 1 *

Section 16: Glossary of Gymnastics Terms

Section 17: Miscellaneous Forms

Section 18: References

Certification Online

This program is unique in that a companion program to this manual exists online at: http://www.gymcert.com/. This program also is available in CD format which has streaming video of the skills that are taught at this level.

The online version of Gymnastics: Boys Level 1 Coaches Certification Manual contains additional information as well as streaming videos that demonstrate each of the skills in Level 1, Level 2 and Level 3 certification.

Congratulations on your decision to improve your knowledge and skills as a gymnastics instructor, now let's get started!

SECTION 2

Legal Responsibilities of the Gymnastics Instructor

- "According to the National Youth Sports Foundation, 3.5 million children suffer from sports-related injuries each year."[2]

- "According to a new study by doctors, about 8 out of 10 of the kids who don't get hurt know the safety rules."[3]

Currently, we live in a litigious society. People sue for very little reason in the hopes of making big money.

As a gymnastics instructor you have been given the most precious commodity of all to safeguard; a human life. Today, more so than the past, parents are checking into the credentials of those who have control over any aspect of their child's life. You need to be prepared. If you want to call yourself a gymnastics instructor, you must be willing to learn and continue to upgrade your knowledge of correct and safe teaching methods.

The Most Important Questions

The most important questions a gymnastics instructor should be able to answer at any time while teaching young gymnasts are:

1. Is the gymnastics equipment properly set up, and is the surrounding gymnastics area prepared for the safe performance of gymnastics skills?

2. Is the gymnast physically prepared to do the skill? (I.E. appropriate strength, flexibility, spatial awareness, timing, and consistency of action)

---

[2] Dr. Hank Clever, Special to the St. Charles County Post, TAKE THESE PRECAUTIONS TO PROTECT CHILDREN FROM SPORTS-RELATED INJURIES., St. Louis Post-Dispatch, 06-10-2002, pp10.
[3] Elizabeth Siris, *Play Smart!.*, Time for Kids, 10-05-2001, pp2+.

3. Does the gymnast understand exactly what is expected of him in the performance of the skill?

4. Is the gymnast mentally prepared to do the skill?

5. Is the instructor properly prepared to teach the skill?

This includes an awareness of:
- Proper progressions of gymnastics skills.
- Appropriate lesson plans.
- How to safely spot the gymnast.
- How to adapt technique based on gymnast size, shape, and physical ability.

6. Has the instructor received training and certification in CPR and First Aid?

7. Has the instructor specifically warned each gymnast of the potential risks and hazards posed in the skills being taught, and has the instructor received feedback from the gymnast indicating the gymnast understands the risk?

The reality of life

The reality is that you can do your job as a gymnastics instructor to the best of your ability and still find yourself involved in litigation if a child under your care is injured.

Some people will initiate lawsuits in the hope of a big payoff; others sincerely need the money to pay medical expenses related to the injury. The amount of money being sought in a lawsuit is usually more than the average coach has the ability to pay.

As the defendant (person being sued) in a lawsuit, it will be your job to prove the plaintiff's (people suing you) allegations about your conduct before during and after the accident were not negligent (substandard conduct for any reasonable / professional coach).

Duty, Breach of Duty, and Cause

In any case in which the plaintiff claims negligence, there must be proof that you had a duty to act in a certain manner, that you breached or failed to carry out that duty, and as such your breach of duty was one of the primary or "proximate" causes of the accident. If that can be established, you may be liable for damages (payment of bills, financial settlement) to the plaintiff. In most cases, your lawyer will attempt to reduce your liability by establishing comparative negligence, which means that if anyone else had any part in causing the accident the cost of paying the award would be split among all those found negligent, depending on the percentage of their involvement.

Legal Duties of Coaches [4]

1. Supervise the activity closely.
2. Properly plan the activity.
3. Provide proper instruction.
4. Provide a safe physical environment.
5. Provide adequate and proper equipment.
6. Warn of inherent risks.
7. Provide appropriate emergency assistance.
8. Keep informed.
9. Know your students.
10. Keep adequate records.

The duty is yours

While this manual will educate and help to guide you, the responsibility for any child placed in your care as gymnastics professional is yours. It is up to you to fulfill the role of a reasonable and prudent professional gymnastics instructor. Always teach in progression. Progressions are step-by-step, logical sequences of skills and drills. Never leave a class unsupervised not even to take a bathroom break or phone call. Call over another instructor or staff member to supervise or take over your class if you have to leave the area for any reason! In the following pages, you will be introduced to basic concepts in planning classes, training skills, and especially keeping safe the young gymnasts, you are charged with. This certification program and this manual is not the end, but the first step in your journey as a gymnastics professional.

Assumption of Risk

Participation in gymnastics involves motion, rotation, and height in a unique environment and as such carries with it a reasonable amount of risk.

Ways of warning participants of inherent risks are by:
- posting safety rules in the gym and parents waiting/observation areas
- printing rules and policies on brochures, handouts and registration forms
- parents/gymnasts sign waivers or participation agreements that specifically state the inherent risks. Recommend to give a copy to the parent to keep.
- verbally describing potential risks and potential causes for injury for a new skill
- watching videos of the skill and discussing risks

---

[4] Condensed from Figure 2.1 – "Legal Duties of Coaches" from USA Gymnastics Safety Handbook, Indianapolis: USAG Publications, 1998 Edition.

SECTION 3

Basic Gymnastics Technique

In this chapter, you will get a brief overview of basic gymnastics techniques[5]. While not a substitute for mentoring from an accomplished coach or the valuable knowledge you can gain by attending gymnastics clinics and seminars, you will be presented with some of the basic principles that will help you analyze gymnastics skills performed by your gymnasts and provide you with insights into making suggestions for improving the skill.

There are several interlocking concepts. Unfortunately, we live in a mundane linear dimension that allows the presentation of only one concept at a time. Because of this limitation, some topics may not seem readily applicable. Have patience and by the end of the discussion, you will see how they all fit together.

Overview of the concepts

- Strength & Flexibility
- Body Lines / Segmentation
- Center of gravity / Body shapes: mesomorph, ectomorph, endomorph.
- Base of support.
- Lines of force from gravity.
- Vectors of force – horizontal / vertical & angular momentum.
- Pattern of errors: talking less and coaching more.
- Feedback: Senseless cheerleading or positive direction?
- Fear: unconscious body knowledge & its effect on technique.

Okay, let's begin.

---

[5] Feeney, Rik. Basic Gymnastics Techniques: Vault, Bars, Beam, and Floor. Perry, FL: Richardson Publishing, 2002.

Strength & Flexibility

Strength

Let's not belabor the point, especially because it is spoken to directly in the Conditioning chapter, but strength and flexibility are two critical factors toward the successful acquisition of new gymnastics skills. Strength supplies the power for a pull up on bars, the tightness of leg and torso muscles to effectively punch off a springboard on vault, and the ability to keep the arms straight on a back handspring saving a gymnast from landing in a nose pose.

There is only one way to get strength and that is through a series of exercises (see Conditioning Level 1) that progressively increase the level of resistance or workload on the gymnast's muscles. A proper strength program will take into account all the muscles of the body with special emphasis on the upper body and abdominal muscles of the young gymnast.

Why upper body? Because most young children are active with bike riding, running in the school yard, playing soccer, and walking all over the neighborhood. Their legs are in much better shape because they are used all the time. You don't often see young children getting around by running on their hands or log rolling down the street, so the emphasis should probably be on upper body and abdominal muscles.

Flexibility

Flexibility can be described as having the ability to move a body segment in the widest range of motion possible while maintaining control and joint stability. It is important to note that flexibility is specific to each joint in the body. That means that because the right ankle has a certain range of motion does not mean the left ankle will have the same range of motion. Previous injuries, bone defect, tightness of the ligaments and tendons crossing the joint all have an effect on its flexibility or range of motion. Have your gymnasts show you their right and left splits. It is not uncommon that one side is better than the other, but marked differences in flexibility could be a warning of future injury.

While not universal, you may find that because of the time spent running, biking, and playing that gymnasts are more flexible in the upper body and tighter in the legs. Whatever the case, plan according to the needs of your class.

An overall goal for your gymnasts is to be as strong as possible through the widest range of motion. (See Flexibility skills in the Floor Exercise section.)

Body Lines / Segmentation

Segmentation is a fancy way of describing the lines the body creates when doing gymnastics skills. The number of lines created while attempting a gymnastics skill can mean success or failure. The least number of lines visible in a gymnast's body, the better the technique, and the higher the chance of completing the skill correctly. In the illustrations below you can see the body create three major lines starting from one graceful line in stretch position, to two major body lines in standing pike, and three lines in a seated tuck.

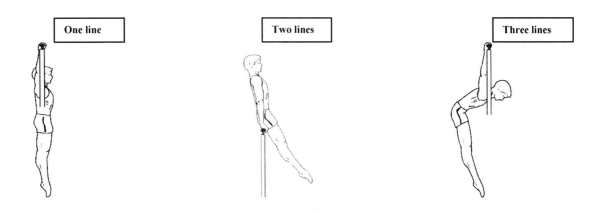

The more lines the body has (potentially up to 7 lines) the more the gymnast has to focus on control at each joint. Each attempt will vary in the amount of bend he has in each joint making a consistency of performance next to impossible. For example, kicking up to a handstand there should be only two major lines; the body with arms stretched above the head, and the one leg stepping forward with a straight knee coming together with the other leg to end in one line again at the handstand. Most gymnasts practice kicking up to a handstand by bending the front knee; how much they bend the knee on each attempt varies. The constant variation makes locking into a tight body handstand more difficult.

On the other hand, maybe the child is too inflexible to kick up with a straight leg and would pull a muscle if he tried. In that case, we are back to conditioning; specifically flexibility.

You will find as we skim through these basic techniques that they are all inextricably woven together; the lack of any one having a demonstrable consequence on technique. The body lines will come into focus more in the following concepts.

Center of gravity / Body shapes: mesomorph, ectomorph, endomorph.

The center of gravity in any geometric figure is usually the geometric center of the object. (The cross marks the geometric center of gravity in the diamond, octagon, and triangle.)

The "center of gravity" is usually considered to be that spot about which the weight of an object is equally divided or balanced. Remember in elementary school, taking your ruler and putting your pencil through the middle hole to make a helicopter? That middle hole was the center of gravity and the point about which the ruler rotated to create the helicopter blades.

The center of gravity for a gymnast is dependent on the body type and size. There are generally three distinct body types: the ectomorph, the endomorph, and the mesomorph. Ectomorphs tend to be thin with almost sticklike bodies. Endomorphs tend to be more pear-shaped with most of their weight in the lower body.
Mesomorphs tend to be muscular and carry more of their weight in their upper body (think of Arnold Schwartzenegger).

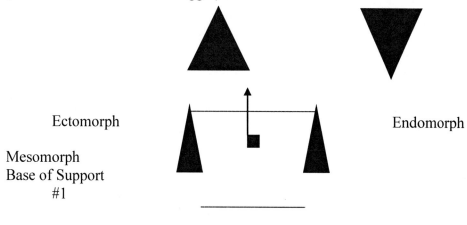

Ectomorph   Endomorph

Mesomorph
Base of Support
#1

Base of Support & Center of Gravity

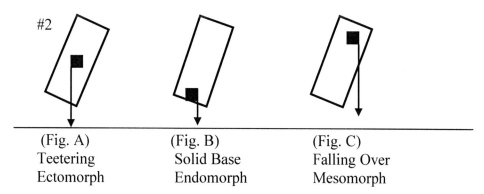

(Fig. A)	(Fig. B)	(Fig. C)
Teetering	Solid Base	Falling Over
Ectomorph	Endomorph	Mesomorph

Base of support.

Your base of support and the base of support of any object is made up of the area directly under the support system. Your legs are your support system, a football player in a 3-point stance uses both legs and one arm as a support system, and the four legs under your table are a support system. In picture #1, the elongated triangles represent your feet. The dotted line that runs from toe to toe and heel to heel represents the front and back line of your base of support. The total area encompassed by your feet and within the two lines is your base of support.

Base of Support & Center of Gravity

Gravitational forces are perpendicular to the planet, that is, like the arrows in figure #2 the force goes straight down. When you are standing in a balanced position the line of force from gravity would go straight down through the middle of your head and directly through the middle of your base of support and represents your center of gravity. In picture #2, the square dot in Figure A represents your center of gravity when you are standing still in a balanced position. Should you lean forward and move your center of gravity toward the front line of your base of support you will begin to fall over. As the arrow in Figure C represents, when your center of gravity gets outside your base of support you have two choices; 1) take a step to catch your balance, or, 2) fall flat on your face.

In large part, the key to running fast on vault is to lose your balance quicker and quicker by leaning forward and keeping your center of gravity outside the front line of your base of support.

Developing techniques based on body size is why the center of gravity is so important in this discussion. Remember, an ectomorph is built like a stick so his center of gravity will be dead center in his body, whereas the endomorph has most of his weight in the lower part of his body, so his center of gravity will be much lower. The mesomorph tends to have a higher center of gravity because of more upper body weight.

Since many aspects of gymnastics involve turning upside down quickly or fast rotation around the body's center of gravity, it is important to adapt techniques for different body types.

Think of a front handspring vault over the horse. The key is to run fast, punch off the board, and invert the body as quickly as possible. Which gymnast would ask to lean forward on the board; which one would you tell to lean backward; and which would you tell to stand up straight?

In Picture #2 (page 9), there are three identical boxes. In each is placed a 50-pound weight that represents the box's center of gravity. If we draw a line straight down like the force of gravity we can see that the box on the far left representing the ectomorph has the center of gravity just touching the front line of the base of support in a precarious balance. The endomorph in the second box has his center of gravity clearly within his base of support; no chance of his falling over. The mesomorph on the far right has his center of gravity well outside his base of support and will definitely tip over and fall.

Assuming the board is set correctly for the gymnast's height and ability, and a smoothly accelerating run with a good punch; you would probably have the ectomorph stand up on the board, the endomorph lean forward on the board, and the mesomorph lean slightly backward to allow sufficient time for the gymnast to extend his body before contact with the horse / vault table.

The roles are reversed on beam where the endomorph has an advantage with balance because of his lower center of gravity and the mesomorph is constantly in danger of falling off because of his higher center of gravity.

Let's see if we can pull a few of these concepts together; body lines, lines of force, and center of gravity. Remember that force always travels in a straight line within the body. If you were standing in front of me with your arms straight out and I pushed on your hands; the force would go straight through your arms and into your body causing you to be pushed backwards. If I did the same push on your arms and you bent your elbows, the force that would have gone through your body now goes out into empty air. If you think no force is going out the elbow, try sticking your face behind someone doing this drill and I guarantee you will get a severe smack in the mouth.

To conserve power in a particular direction for a gymnastics skill, instruct the gymnast to use the least number of body segments, and to keep those segments in one unbroken line (of course, this changes depending on whether the skill is stylized with a tuck, pike, or some other required position). To use that force effectively for rotation you must set the takeoff angle based on the particular center of gravity of the gymnast in question.

Vectors of force – horizontal / vertical & angular momentum

Of course, that leads us into vectors of force, which is a fancy way of saying the direction of force. The direction of force has two components; horizontal and vertical. Anything moving horizontally is going side to side like the type on this page. Anything moving vertically is going straight up. All gymnastics skills are made up of some combination of horizontal and vertical movement. The specific skill determines which of these components, horizontal or vertical, is the most important in the skill and therefore the angle of takeoff that you need to train.

For instance, a back tuck somersault is a skill that displays vertical lift. A round off and three back handsprings would highlight horizontal velocity. Yet, both skills still have some portion of the opposing quality. A backward somersault does have some horizontal or backward travel, and a back handspring has some vertical lift. Coaching the takeoff angle determines what skill the gymnast performs. If a gymnast lands with his feet directly under his and his body is in a nice tight line the resulting rebound will take his up and some of his horizontal momentum will take his back, but he will primarily be blocking for a somersault takeoff. If he does a round off and snaps his feet through to land well in front of his hips and the body is in a nice hollow line, he will be propelled primarily backward, presumably to do a back handspring.

Again, the variations in takeoff need to take into account body shape regarding center of gravity, speed of the motion, the strength of the gymnast in maintaining body lines, and the flexibility of the body parts in question to reach that particular range of motion. As you can see from this brief discussion, there is no one technique fits all. As the coach you will have to adapt the techniques based on the gymnast's conditioning, understanding of the skill, and mental preparation and be prepared to continually refine the technique as the gymnast grows physically and mentally.

To Summarize:

Is the gymnast strong enough to generate and maintain the proper body line for the skill?

Is the gymnast flexible enough to achieve the proper body line without injury?

Have you adapted the takeoff angle of the skill to the body type, conditioning level, and sequential process of the skill?

Can the gymnast control (with or without help) the processional effects of each attempt (I.E. land safely)?

If you can apply each of the techniques mentioned in this chapter, you will be well on your way to developing talented gymnasts.

Pattern of errors

Most coaches like to *over* correct thus giving gymnasts several solutions to fix the problems with his last skill attempt. "Your legs were bent." "You didn't run fast enough, the turn was too early, your eyes are crossed, and your left earlobe is too small." The gymnast didn't hear anything past the first comment.

On a single attempt, the arms might have been bent, but on the next several attempts, they are perfectly straight; just the way you want them. The key to effective coaching is to look for a "pattern of errors." Practice giving the gymnast just one coaching tip and then let his practice a few times and see if he makes the same mistake each time or a different one each time. If he is making a different one each time, he is learning. If he is making the same mistake repeatedly, it is time to offer a coaching cue or drill to remedy the situation.

Feedback: Senseless cheerleading or positive direction?

"Good" "Better" "Oh, that's wonderful!" "Great!"

The gymnast just took four turns and the above comments were all he heard. What did he learn? Obviously, he is best thing since music videos, but he didn't pick up a thing that would help his to refine his gymnastics technique. Don't get me wrong, everyone needs a pat on the back, but the key is to give your students a constructive correction in a positive encouraging way. In fact, psychologists call it the theory of "limited reward." Anything that consistently and effortlessly produces a reward, verbal or otherwise, becomes meaningless and boring. Can you imagine having your gymnasts attempt a skill 20 times during the class and after each attempt you are saying some version of "that's better!" I believe that it is important to find many different ways of saying that's wonderful. Change your tone of voice and words often. Be positive and encouraging to all of your students.

It may be better to give positive oriented directions after every few skill attempts. For instance, if I say don't think of an elephant, the chance is very good that a picture of an elephant popped into your mind anyway. When you as a coach say, "don't bend your legs," the gymnast goes away focusing on a mental picture of bent legs. The appropriate comment would be "Next time, keep your legs straight." Now the gymnast has a mental picture of straight legs. Always tell the gymnast what you want them to do on the next attempt. Berating a gymnast for a skill that is done is a waste of time. A good example for a job well done would be to give your gymnast a high five and verbal praise. Positive oriented direction is the best method for creating constructive change.

Fear: unconscious body knowledge & its effect on technique.

The last factor to consider in this chapter is fear and its affect on attempting gymnastics skills. First off, being scared is a normal reaction to new and difficult skills. Remember, that many of the skills now taught in normal classes were considered Olympic level skills less than 30 years ago.

The key to dealing with fear in the gymnast is to acknowledge it and allow the gymnast to have that fear; it is a valid response. The gymnast might be scared on the first attempt; the gymnast might continue to be scared on the 500th attempt. The key is channeling the energy created by the fear into positively oriented action steps. Break the skill down to its component parts and slowly put it back together again, allowing the gymnast plenty of success at each step. When the time comes to integrate the drills into a whole skill or combination, be there to spot the gymnast safely through the maneuver. Continue spotting while creating incremental successes that help the gymnast to eventually obtain the self-confidence to do it on his own.

One thing you will soon realize is that each gymnast has an "unconscious body knowledge" that is a safety mechanism that plays havoc with gymnastic technique. For instance, a gymnast attempts a front handspring. Without consciously thinking about it, he bends his knees to get over, because bending the knees shortens the body's radius causing it to rotate faster so he will land on his feet. Landing on his feet is far better than landing on his back. The only cure for unconscious body knowledge is to create situations where the gymnast feels secure, like with a spot, or on a tumble tramp, in a spotting belt, off a higher stack of mats, anything that will enable his to escape injury.

Of course, most attacks of unconscious body knowledge taking over a gymnast only occur in those gymnasts attempting skills that are beyond their current stage of fitness, technical awareness, and mental preparation. We know that won't happen when you coach.

Each of the techniques presented are applicable to the Floor Exercise, Pommel Horse, Still Rings, Vault, Parallel Bars, and High Bar skills listed in the Gymnastics: Boys Level 1 Coaches Certification Manual.

SECTION 4

Safety in a Gymnastics Program

The most important consideration in the sport of gymnastics is **Safety.** It is the instructor's responsibility to provide a safe environment. This chapter will only scratch the surface of the most important areas. For more extensive and thorough coverage purchase a copy of the ***USAG Safety Manual[6] or USAG Risk Management Manual.***

To review from the introduction, to prevent accidents and reduce risk the instructor must constantly ask himself the following questions when planning and teaching:

1. Is the equipment properly set up, and is the surrounding area prepared for the performance of gymnastics skills?

Heather Maynez - Photographer

2. Is the gymnast mentally and physically ready, and does the gymnast understand exactly what is expected of him or his in the performance of the skill? To make sure the gymnast understands a technique you should have the gymnast tell you in his own words what you want his to do.

3. Has the coach properly prepared himself or herself to teach the skill by using proper progressions, lesson plans, and learning the correct spotting techniques?

Environmental Considerations

Is the equipment properly set up, and is the surrounding area prepared for the performance of gymnastics skills?

Before the performance of any gymnastics skill, the instructor should check the workout area to be sure that the gymnastics apparatus and appropriate matting is properly set up for the performance of the gymnastics skill. In order to do this properly, it is recommended that the instructor arrive at least 15 minutes before their first class of the day. At this time you can plan for proper traffic flow and set up any additional matting or teaching aids that may be needed.

---

[6] Whitlock, Steve (editor). <u>USA Gymnastics Safety Handbook</u>. Indianapolis: USAG Publications, 1998.

Items to Check:

1. Mats appropriate to the gymnastics skill being attempted should be in place under the apparatus being used by the gymnast (s).   What is appropriate may vary depending on the competence of the performer, the knowledge of the instructor, and other activities taking place in the gym at the same time. A forward roll on the floor will not need a stack of mats 3 feet high, however, attempting the forward roll on the rings or parallel bars a novice may need (and want!) just that as well as a spot from the instructor.

2. The instructor and the gymnast should make sure the equipment is properly adjusted and secured at the dimensions appropriate to the gymnast performing.

The high bar, parallel bars, rings, and vault may be adjusted in height (and width and height on parallel bars) to accommodate the various sizes of the gymnasts. The class gymnast will set equipment according to preference and appropriate to the skill being performed. Once a setting has been determined, all fasteners and tightening devices should be securely set. The instructor should check to make sure the equipment is properly set before allowing any skills to be practiced.

The task of setting gymnastics equipment can be a risky venture. Unnecessary accidents occur in the gym when instructors and gymnasts who are unfamiliar with the mechanisms of the different apparatus attempt to adjust them without qualified assistance. If you are unfamiliar with the equipment, ask an experienced instructor or the club owner / program director to demonstrate how to set the equipment properly and safely.

The instructor should help the gymnast set the equipment according to their body size and skill level. **Note:** Settings for a gymnast will change as he becomes more proficient in the skill. For example, the springboard may be moved farther away on vault as the gymnast learns to run faster, or as the gymnast grows physically, or adapts to changing techniques, or begins training new levels of gymnastics skills.

Safety Notes:

Bars:
A. Always release the tension on the cables first before attempting to raise or lower a bar or before attempting to adjust the width of the bars. Usually, it is a good idea to tighten the back cables first, then the front cables to make sure the bars are properly aligned and not cockeyed.
B. When raising or lowering the bars keep your hands off the piston and on the rail itself. Holding the piston right where it adjusts up and down could be risky if the bar suddenly slips and tears a chunk of skin out of your hand. In addition, never stand with your shoulder under the bar rail. If it should suddenly drop, it could hit a gymnast in the head, or an instructor in the shoulder causing serious injury.

C. Never jump or hang on a piece of equipment in an attempt to get it to   move. Keep gymnasts away from the apparatus until it is adjusted and secured. Fun-loving but unaware children may jump on the bar while you are setting it. To avoid stripping the screws on tighteners, use only the pressure you can apply with your thumb on one end and first two fingers of the same hand on the other end. You don't have to kill it to tighten it.

Parallel Bars:

A. There is basically one method for adjusting the parallel bars and that is by adjusting the pistons on the sides of the support base. This is where you adjust the width and the height of the bars. When raising or lowering the bars keep your hands off the piston and on the rail itself. Holding the piston right where it adjusts up and down could be risky if the bar suddenly slips and tears a chunk of skin out of your hand.

B. In addition, never stand with your shoulder under the bar rail. If it should suddenly drop, it could hit a gymnast in the head, or an instructor in the shoulder causing serious injury.

C. Never jump or hang on a piece of equipment in an attempt to get it to move.

D. Keep gymnasts away from the apparatus until it is adjusted and secured. Fun-loving but unaware children may jump on the bar while you are setting it. Always be prepared for this and instruct them not to touch the apparatus until you are done adjusting it.

E. To avoid stripping the screws on lighteners, use only the pressure you can apply with your thumb on one end and first two fingers of the same hand on the other end. Try not to over tighten it.

F. Always build up mats under the parallel bars. It is sometimes easier to build up then to lower the bars. Either way is acceptable.

Vault:

A. Vault has similar pistons to the bars along with a pull pin. When raising or lowering the vault keep your hands off the piston. Most vault horses have springs in the piston, which make raising and lowering the vault top relatively easy. Sometimes when one side is much higher than the other, the vault will stick on the lower side. Simply lower the higher side a few notches until both sides can rise at the same time. If the pistons consistently stick while raising and lowering, ask your club owner or program director to lubricate the piston.

B. Holding the piston right where it adjusts up and down could be risky if the vault top suddenly slips and tears a chunk of skin out of your hand. In addition, it is quite easy for your hand and wrist to get caught between the piston and the horse top causing injury.

C. Never jump or hang on the vault in an attempt to get it to move.

Springboards:

Springboards are devices designed to take the speed and power of a run and re-direct it for the performance of a skill. A brand new board may be quite stiff and hard to bounce off for younger and lighter gymnasts. Some clubs may substitute mini-tramps or mini-tramps shaped like vault boards for recreational gymnasts or the instructor may remove some springs. Be sure the springboard has the right number of springs for the weight and power of the gymnast using it, or he may bottom-out the board, which could cause injury to the legs and lower back.

- The area where the skill is being performed should be clear of obstructions, other pieces of equipment, or parts of the building.

- The traffic flow from other gymnasts on other events should be routed so they do not interfere with the performance of the skill.

- The gym should be well lit, and any sound systems present should not be overpowering to the extent that directions cannot be heard.

Gymnast Preparation

Is the gymnast mentally and physically ready, and does the gymnast understand exactly what is expected of his in the performance of the skill?

The instructor decides whether a gymnast is prepared to do a particular gymnastics skill by answering these three questions:

1. Is the gymnast physically prepared to do the skill? (i.e. appropriate levels of strength and/or flexibility)

2. Is the gymnast aware of the timing and sequence of events that must occur to perform the skill successfully, and can the gymnast feed that information back to the instructor?

3. Is the gymnast mentally prepared to do the skill? (either alone or with assistance?)

Gymnast Physical Preparation

For a gymnast to perform a skill, a certain level of strength and flexibility must first be achieved. The first area, strength, is obvious. If a gymnast is unable to do even one push up on the floor the chance is very good the gymnast will fall flat on his head when attempting a handstand. Likewise, a lack of flexibility could cause a painful tear in a muscle when attempting a dynamic gymnastics skill.

The instructor may on occasion lift the gymnast through the skill even when the child does not have the ability to do the skill alone. The purpose is to help familiarize the gymnast with the physical needs of the skill, as well as to develop spatial awareness during the performance of the skill, but this should not take the place of proper conditioning. Proper conditioning for gymnastics consists primarily of strength and flexibility. (see Conditioning: Strength & Flexibility)

Gymnast Technical Preparation

Gymnasts should be able to explain in their own words exactly what they are supposed to do to perform the skill, and when they are supposed to do it. If there is any question about proper procedure, the gymnast should stop and get further information from the instructor. Many times fear at performing the skill alone can be traced back to a lack of understanding of the mechanics of the skill.

It is especially important that the instructor make sure that the gymnast is actually paying attention. Ask for feedback by posing questions with multiple answers or get the class as a whole to respond. Correct obvious errors without making anyone "wrong." If an inappropriate reply is made say, "well, that's certainly one answer, but how about…" and then supply the right answer and the chance for the gymnast to save face in front of his peers.

Gymnast Mental Preparation

The area of mental preparation is the most difficult to ascertain because of the many differing personalities in the class. It is usually easy to determine whether the novice gymnast is ready or whether he is scared and needs additional help. However, with the more advanced beginner gymnast, who wants to get the skill and possibly to please his instructors, it may not be as easy to determine whether the gymnast is ready to do a skill, even when the gymnast is being spotted. Some of the more advanced of beginner skills can be scary even when the instructor is standing there to protect the gymnast. It is important for the instructor and the gymnast to be sure the skill will be performed when the gymnast says it will. Having to change spotting techniques mid-trick and perform what author, Wm. A. Sands[7] refers to as a "rescue

---

[7] Sands, Wm. A. How Effective is Rescue Spotting? *Technique*, October 1996, Vol. 16, No. 9.

spot[8]" because a gymnast "chickens out" can be very dangerous for both the instructor and the gymnast.

The key is clear communication between the gymnast and the instructor. If there is ever any doubt, the gymnast should always ask to have another spot. It may even be necessary to break the skill down again and relearn it. Again, according to Sands from his book, *Coaching Women's Gymnastics*[9], "One of the best guidelines you can adopt is to ask yourself, 'Can the gymnast do this skill even if he makes the worst possible mistake he is likely to make? If he really blows it, can he still complete the skill successfully enough to avoid injury or a fearful situation?' If the answer to this is 'yes,' then go ahead and try one" (131).

Note: Some gymnasts may not attempt a particular skill because they do not trust their spotters. Trust in a particular instructor's spotting ability is something that must be earned. Once earned, an instructor can never abuse this trust, the instructor must always be there when the gymnast needs help or the gymnast will not give the instructor a second chance. (See the section on Spotting for more information.)

Instructor's Preparation (Whole/Part/Whole Method)

The instructor prepares for a gymnast to do gymnastics skill by breaking the skill down into its smallest parts and teaching each of these parts in a way that enables the gymnast to progress in ability toward the skill desired.

Depending on a particular gymnast's style of learning the instructor will present the information verbally (auditory), physically (kinesthetic), or through demonstration (visual). Ideally, each of these methods should be used in concert with the focus on that individual's style.

The instructor learns how to teach skills by attending gymnastics clinics and seminars or by working with another instructor to become familiar with the techniques necessary for teaching the skill.

An instructor demonstrates preparation by asking the gymnast to relay his or his understanding of the skill and then describing to the gymnast how the skill will be spotted. The instructor will answer any questions the gymnast may have until the

---

[8] A "rescue spot" occurs when a sudden and unexpected change occurs in the performance of the skill, causing the instructor to mentally take the time to understand what has happened and then choose a response while the gymnast is falling. More often than not, the gymnast hits the floor before the coach can react.

[9] Sands, Wm. A. <u>Coaching Women's Gymnastics</u>. Champaign, Il: Human Kinetics, 1984.

gymnast is satisfied and feels ready to attempt the skill. Any inherent risks in the skill should be explained to gymnast before the actual performance of the skill.

Factors Affecting Your Lesson Plan

- Class Size: Depends on the type of class being taught.
  a) preschool – 4 to 6 gymnasts
  b) beginner – 6 to 10 gymnasts
  c) Intermediate / Advanced – 6 to 10 gymnasts
  d) Cheerleaders / Tumblers – 10 to 15

- Level of supervision: General vs. Specific

The key to maintaining appropriate levels of safety at all times is adequate supervision of the activity. It must never be assumed that children will do what is "right" all the time. Being young, and wanting to have fun, a child may not realize the potential danger in some of his activities or "horseplay" around gymnastics equipment. There are two basic types of supervision, general and specific.

General Supervision

This is where an instructor(s) keep watch over a group activity, such as tumbling with a group of gymnasts, or overseeing several gymnasts working on the balance beam. This type of supervision is appropriate when the gymnasts are working on skills they have become proficient in doing alone.

Specific Supervision

Specific supervision is necessary when a gymnast is attempting a new and/or difficult skill for the first time. Specific supervision is also necessary on certain pieces of apparatus where the chance of injury is high because of the nature of the equipment, such as the trampoline, mini-tramp, tumble tramp, and the pit.

- Equipment available for training

Depending on the day and time, you may have the gym to yourself, or it could be packed wall to wall with gymnast in several different classes limiting your ability to rotate or use equipment freely.

- Instructor's knowledge of gymnastics techniques and spotting skills.

Attire

Gymnastics instructors are professionals and therefore are considered role models in their profession. Proper work-out clothing should be worn by both the instructor and the gymnast. Clothing should be free of snaps, large buttons, clasps and belts. Those items could get in the way while spotting and/or executing a skill. Clothing should be comfortable and easy to move in. Proper gymnastics apparel is recommended. Gym shorts and T-shirts for boys and leotards for female class students are acceptable. Street clothes like blue jeans are not considered proper work-out apparel for instructors or students.

Jewelry is not recommended at any time. Candy and gum have no place in the gymnastics environment. Long hair should be neat and properly tied back. Vision should not be impaired by hair falling into eyes or in front of face. Street shoes should not be worn in the gymnastics studio. Gymnastics shoes/slippers, gym shoes, socks, or bare feet are acceptable in the gymnastics class.

2004 USA Olympian Brett McClure
Photo courtesy of Heather Maynez

Lesson Plans

A basic lesson plan includes: *(for a 1-hour class)*
- 0:00 – 0:07   Cardio-warm up & Stretching
- 0:07 – 0:22   Two to three events   15
- 0:22 – 0:37   of activity that review   minute
- 0:37 – 0:52   and present new skills.   rotations.
- 0:52 – 1:00   Fun activity and warm down.

Class Styles

Master Lesson:
- The instructor may take the whole class and teach a particular skill on a gymnastics event, after which the class will be broken into groups to work with specific instructors to learn the skill.

Group Rotations:
- The class may be broken into different groups and rotate through the gym spending a certain amount of time working on each apparatus and then rotating to the instructor on the next event. Sometimes the instructor may rotate with the group.

Circuit Training:
- Specific skills and drills may be set up at each apparatus that a gymnast must do after working the main skill with the instructor. Each of these drills and/or skills are designed to enhance the progress of the gymnast in one particular gymnastics skill or physical development area.

Skill Progressions

Progressions are gymnastics skills broken down in ability level from the simplest to the most difficult. An appropriate program of training will make use of a series of well thought out progressions to make sure the learning is appropriate in all phases of the gymnastics experience. Included within the text of this book is a series of progressions on all the events (Floor Exercise, Pommel Horse, Still Rings, Vault, Parallel Bars, and High Bar) with additional information on trampoline, conditioning, and body positions.

As an instructor, you will use these progressions as goals for your class and subsequently elements of your lesson plans. Skill progressions are used in the following ways in your lesson plan:

1. Teach the most basic form of the skill.
2. Teach variations of the basic skill.
3. Put the skill and/or its variations into sequences of 2-3 skills.

Obviously, unless you have a child prodigy in class, most of your gymnasts will not learn the skill right away. They will need to practice it over and over, which can get repetitive.

How to vary skills:

- **Add a:** tuck, squat, pike, straddle, layout, or stretch position to it.

- **Start from:** stretch position, attention, another skill, a stand, a walk, from a run, skip, jump, or wiggle.

- **Finish** in a finish pose or salute.

- Do the skill from the **left** and the **right.**

- Do it going **up** and going **down**.

- **Add a** 1/4, 1/2, 1/1, **turn** to the skill.

- **Attempt it ?** number of times, or **make it ?** number of times.

- **Start** in one spot and **finish** in another.

- Go **over, under, or through** something.

- Create a complete **circuit** of skills.

- Do it on **one leg, two legs**, or **alternate**.

- Do it in a **circle, square**, or whatever **shape**. Stay within a **boundary**.

- Impose a **time limit**.

- Give a **reward. (Examples: star, check off, certificate, stamp, ribbon)**

Obviously, you won't apply each of these ideas to every skill on every event. **Safety** is the key word when experimenting with new ideas or techniques. If you are not sure about a new skill or variation you would like to try, always check with the Gym Director, head coach, or club owner for guidance.

Introductory and Periodic Review of the Basics
(a continuing lesson plan)

The purpose of this lesson plan is to familiarize new and returning students with the rules of safety, safe landing procedures, and the appropriate protocol expected of each student during gymnastic training. A successful lesson plan should provide the gymnast with feelings of satisfaction via accomplishment and social approval from their classmates and instructor.

I. Introduction: Introduce yourself and any other staff members that may be present. Inform parents and gymnasts of who does what in the gym for future reference. Discuss briefly basic procedures and policies such as where to put clothes, where parents can sit, make-up classes, holidays, and payment of class fees. Finish with a brief description of this class and its purpose.

II. Warm Up Procedure: Discuss and demonstrate appropriate warm up procedures.

Points to stress regarding stretching: (after cardio-warm up)

1. Be relaxed.
2. Hold the stretch for 30-60 seconds at the point mild tension is felt in the muscle.
3. Absolutely *NO BOUNCING!*
4. Focus attention on the muscle being stretched; visualize the muscle being relaxed; isolate and stretch only that muscle.
5. Breathe slowly and naturally.

III. Safety Rules: Discuss the posted safety rules and any specific guidelines unique to your gym.

IV. Gymnastics Terminology: Define for the parents and gymnasts basic gymnastics terminology on each event. Use floor exercise as your base and teach everyone the basic body positions (I.E. stretch, attention, squat, tuck, pike, straddle, and layout). Show the position both open and closed where applicable. Play a quick game of Simon Says using the different body positions. (see Body Positions on page 47)

V. Evaluation of Floor Basics: This portion of the class should be used to determine each gymnast's capabilities using the basic floor skills: forward roll, backward roll, cartwheel, and handstand. For more advanced gymnasts use the progressions your club has listed for each class level. Keep notes on each gymnast to help determine the appropriate class level. Time permitting you can test each gymnast on other pieces of gymnastics apparatus.

WARNING: If a gymnast is unfamiliar with any skill, including the basics, do not have them just "go for it." A young gymnast throwing himself into a backward roll to impress you could end up straining the tendons on the back of his neck. Sending a gymnast home injured from his first class is not the best first impression. Create situations where the gymnast can attempt the skill without the possibility of injury.

VI. Attitude Training: Unfortunately, in this high tech world children have been brought up to expect immediate gratification of their desires. When these same children are unable to perform a skill correctly the first time, they lose interest and usually don't want to do it anymore.

A major component of our job as gymnastics instructors is to train young gymnasts in how to deal with frustration. Learning to walk, we fell several times before we learned to control our reflexes. Each new gymnast will also have a series of falls or mistakes before they are able to execute each skill correctly. The most important training we can provide is to teach them to keep a positive attitude towards their skill development. **It is not important whether the skill is performed perfectly each time, however, it is important that each attempt is the best they are capable of at that moment.**

Teach your students the words and attitude *"I can't"* are inappropriate and will not be accepted from them during the class. Instead, teach them to say and feel, *"I'll do my best!"* No matter what the outcome, show them that you appreciate their efforts. Help them to concentrate on the rewards of success, rather than the penalties of failure.

VII. Conclusion: You may have time to test on other pieces of equipment, as well as some strength and flexibility testing. If not, simply make that your next lesson plan for each of the gymnasts involved.

In a Perfect World...

In a perfect world you could also test strength and flexibility and demonstrate the *"Safety Landing Drills"* during the introductory class. Time does not always permit that luxury so make sure to add it into regularly scheduled classes at specific intervals during the year.

Conditioning:

It is important to test strength and flexibility to help prevent potential injury due to weakness or lack of flexibility. Most novice gymnasts have adequate leg strength, but are weak in the upper body and abdominal region.

Strength Testing You may add or subtract exercises depending on the needs of your program. After several tests you should be able to develop a table of results that will tell you where new students score in relation to the other members of your gym.

Exercises to be tested:
1) Chin ups (palms toward face)
2) Dips on the parallel bars
3) Leg Lifts
4) Standing broad jump

Flexibility Testing Forceful extension of a muscle or joint may cause a strain or tear in the muscle of a gymnast lacking appropriate flexibility. Skills like leg kicks and split leaps are dynamic and take the leg muscles beyond their normal range of motion causing the potential for injury in gymnasts with poor flexibility.

Skills to test for flexibility:
1) Right, left, and middle splits.
2) From a seated pike, bring chest to knees keeping legs straight.
3) Back bends, observing shoulder and lower back flexibility.
4) Passive shoulder flexibility. Lying on your stomach, arms stretched above the head yet touching the ears, lift a small wooden dowel as high as possible above your head without letting your nose come off the floor. Measure the distance from the floor to the dowel.

Make the appropriate comments to parents of individual gymnasts dangerously lacking in either strength or flexibility. Teach the gymnast and parent an appropriate regimen that can also be worked at home to solve this problem.

Safety Landing Drills: Go over the basic *"Safety Landing Drills"* at regular intervals with all the members of your recreational and competitive team programs.

SAFETY LANDING DRILLS

The most important skills to be learned in the sport of gymnastics are the Safety Landing Drills. It is safe to say that on each attempt of a gymnastics skill the gymnast will have a takeoff and a landing. The results of the landing may determine whether the gymnast will want to continue in the sport, or whether he is capable of continuing to participate due to injury.

Given a choice of jumping off a six foot wall onto either cement or a couple of mattresses, most of us would choose to land on the mattresses. Unconsciously, we know that a mattress will absorb the force of our fall and cushion our landing, while landing on cement; the stop is sudden and immediate.

When we land on a surface that gives, such as a landing mat, the force of the fall is distributed over a longer period of time, having less of a destructive effect on the bones and tissues of the body. The principle of distributing force over a longer period, is the key to the following *Safety Landing Drills.* In addition, the body alignment during a landing will play a key role in safe landings.

IMPORTANT: Be sure to practice the following skills initially under the direct supervision of a qualified gymnastics instructor!

No matter which basic landing drill is practiced, emphasize the fact that gymnasts should always attempt (when possible) to land on their feet first! Remember, No Flat-Footed, Stiff-Leg Landings!

The basic safety landing drills are:

1. **Basic Safety Landing Position** (or **SLP**): The basic position requires that the gymnast land from a skill standing mostly upright with the arms up next to the ears (to help protect the neck and head), the knees bent to a 45 degree angle, the stomach sucked in and the lower back is slightly rounded.

It is important to remember that the back is always rounded and the knees are bent on landing otherwise the force of the landing can severely jar the lower back, possibly causing injury.

Note: When practicing these safety landing drills always begin from a low surface such as a folded up mat and progressively work up to a higher surface such as a balance beam. In any case, it is not a good idea to have children under 5 years of age jumping from a surface that is higher than their waist level.

2. SLP with a Side Roll: Whenever over-rotation occurs in landing a skill, this is the position that should be used. To practice, have the gymnast lay on the mat on his back and bring both knees up to the chest, then he will roll completely over in a sideways direction. Next, practice landing in SLP, then go into a sideways roll. Emphasize the fact that the gymnast should always land on their feet first. This drill can be practiced to both sides.

Note: Initially the gymnasts may grab their knees to do the side roll. After a few practices teach them to keep the arms up to protect the head.

3. Backwards SLP: This is the same as the basic SLP except the gymnast will be landing with rotation in a backward direction.

Note: Be sure the gymnast remains upright when jumping backwards. Many gymnasts have a tendency to look down which may cause them to strike their head on the horse or mat they are jumping from. Remember to always work the gymnast up from lower to higher platforms in practicing these skills.

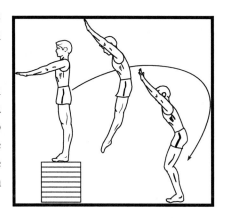

4. Backwards SLP with Rock 'N Roll: First have the gymnast lay on the floor knees and hips bent, lower back rounded, arms up above the head. Have the gymnast practice rocking back and forth in this position.

Next, have the gymnast jump off a raised surface, landing in Backwards SLP, and continue through to the floor rocking backwards (without going over) then rolling back up to a stand. Do not have the gymnast completely roll over, as it is very easy to compress the neck in this position.

The objective of the landing drills is to prevent major injury to the neck, head, and back, however, injury to the extremities is equally unacceptable; though on a priority basis the areas mentioned above should be protected first.

Hand Position: When over-rotating a landing the hands may be placed on the ground to help guide the body into the roll, which will dissipate the force of the fall. The hands should not be used to catch the entire body weight during a fall. Experienced gymnasts may from time to time land and by bending the elbows and absorbing through the shoulders control a fall. This method should be used sparingly as wrist sprains and the like may still occur. Rolling will deliver the force of a fall over a longer period with less chance of injury.

Falling Backwards: The arms should never be placed behind the body with the elbows locked as this invites serious injury to the wrist and elbow, and possible dislocation of the shoulder. If the hands are placed on the floor during a backward rotating fall, the hands should be placed at the sides of the body with the fingers pointing towards the toes so that the elbows can bend as the body rolls backwards.

Horizontal Bar: Each of the drills mentioned may be practiced from a small swing on the bars. Falling from a swing can be a much different experience than falling from other apparatus. A gymnast may come off the bar going in a forward direction while his body rotates backward or vice versa on the bars. Teach the gymnast when dismounting to always release the bar at the peak of the swing, not while still rising in the swing.

Note: When falling from the bars a gymnast who wears grips should never catch his body weight with his hands. The grips placed over the ends of the fingers and strapped to the wrists could break the fingers or bones of the hand upon forceful contact with the mat.

These are the basic safety landing positions. There are other more advanced drills for team members that are neither necessary nor desirable in a class setting. The effectiveness of these Safety Landing Drills will be minimal if they are not practiced on a continuing basis. Habit will make the gymnast land with stiff arms or an arched back, which are dangerous. A station may be set up during the class for gymnasts to practice safe landing drills on their way back into line to break this habit and ensure safe landings.

Sticking your Dismount or Landing

Sticking a dismount is landing on two feet with knees slightly bent, arms extended forward, lower back rounded and no steps. After sticking you should finish in stretched finished position, arms extended upward.

LANDING PROCEDURE FOR PITS (IN-GROUND AND ABOVE-GROUND)

(A pit is like an empty swimming pool filled with loose foam or mats that fill it to the top.)

1. Do not land on head or neck.

2. The gymnast should never land on the stomach or knees.

3. The gymnast should land on his back or side and should not try to land in a support position with arms or legs as this may cause a serious sprain or muscle strain.

4. The gymnast must leave the pit immediately after completing his skill.

5. There is no horseplay at any time around the pit.

6. The gymnast should not attempt any new and/or difficult skill into a pit without the qualified supervision (and possible help) of an instructor.

Note: Initially, these skills should be practiced under the strict supervision of a qualified gymnastics instructor and competent spotter.

Photo Courtesy of Rita Brown

Photo Courtesy of Heather Maynez

Medical Emergencies

First Aid[10]

The following measures are appropriate First Aid for any orthopedic injury such as sprains, strains, and bruises and may be continued for the first two to three days after the injury occurs.

P.R.I.C.E. (Protection, Rest, Ice, Compression, Elevation)

P = PROTECTION from further injury. This includes stopping the class if needed and removing other people or objects from the area that could further jeopardize the gymnast's safety. You may move the gymnast out of harm's way only if you are positive it will not make the injury worse.

NOTE: If an injury exists that requires splinting, such as a serious fracture or dislocation, call 911. The paramedics will splint the injury. **NEVER** try to reduce a fracture or dislocated joint yourself – not even a finger. Serious damage could result. In addition, it is not wise to play doctor and try to make a diagnosis by having the gymnast attempt to move his neck, wiggle his toes, or move any potentially injured body part – this could cause further serious injury. Call 911 or your local emergency hotline and let the professionals handle the situation.

R = REST from function. This means avoiding or limiting use of the body part. It does not mean immobilization unless a fracture or severe tissue tear is present. Gentle movement of the area without external help is sometimes desirable. It helps to prevent stiffness and promote a decrease in swelling. Consult a trainer, therapist, or physician to find out what movement, if any, is appropriate.

I = ICE. Ice shrinks the blood vessels and helps minimize the swelling. Ice is a potent anti-inflammatory agent and decreases pain by numbing the nerves. To apply ice to the injured area, first, place the ice (preferably crushed) in a plastic bag, then put a moist towel between the bag and the skin. Hold them in place over the injured area by wrapping them with an ace bandage. Use the ice treatment for no more than fifteen to twenty minutes at a time, and allow at least thirty minutes between treatments.

---

[10] The text in this *"First Aid"* section was researched and written by Peter F. Clain, M.P.T., and originally appeared in the book *Gymnastics: A Guide for Parents and Athletes.*

Ice applied longer than thirty minutes will actually result in a "rebound" increase in circulation, causing additional swelling and bleeding within the tissue.

NOTE: Never use chemical ice packs over facial injuries or cuts. In addition, never place ice directly on the inside of the elbow, or on the small bone just below the outer part of the knee as serious nerve damage could result.

C = COMPRESSION. Using an Ace bandage, where practical, provides external pressure which helps to minimize swelling and pushes tissue fluids back into the body's circulation, to be drained or "milked out" of the injured region.

A four-inch Ace bandage should be applied, beginning a few inches lower (towards the end of the arm or leg) than the injury site and wrapped (snug, not tight) at a slight diagonal around the area working up to a few inches above the injury. Each "wind" of the bandage should overlap the last one halfway. Make sure all areas are covered. Do not leave any gaps. Tension on the bandage should be slightly greater at the bottom, decreasing towards the top to allow fluid to drain properly back toward the heart.

If numbness, coldness, tingling, or discoloration occurs in the fingers or toes remove the bandage immediately and re-wrap more loosely.

E = ELEVATION. When possible, keep the injured region higher than the chest, or as high as safely possible. This allows gravity to help drain the swelling. Elevation is probably the single most important and effective method in decreasing excess swelling.

Combining Ice, Compression, and Elevation enhances the benefits of each in reducing swelling.

Crack!

There is no mistake about it, a serious injury has just occurred. What you do now can make a big difference in how well or even if the gymnast will fully recover.

Suggestion #1: Make sure you do not become the next victim.

We cannot possibly relate every potential situation for injury, but one of the basic tenets of first aid is not to place yourself in jeopardy or you will be of no use to the injured person. If helping this person will in any way put you at risk call 911 or your local emergency phone numbers and get the professionals there right away.

Suggestion # 2: Get training and certification in First Aid and CPR.

We cannot and would not suggest how you can care for a seriously injured person if you have not been properly trained. The only people who can do that are paramedics, physicians, certified athletic trainers, and physical therapists. Contact the American Red Cross and / or the American Heart Association for information on First Aid and CPR courses.

Suggestion # 3: Call the professionals.

In any situation where you can obviously see a bone is broken, a gymnast has lost consciousness and/or feeling in any part of his body, or is simply unresponsive or incoherent, or has injured any portion of his head, neck, or spine you need to call 911 or the local equivalent immediately.

You might think of yourself as the hero at the moment, but months later in the courtroom you may be the one held liable for damages in a lawsuit. Cover yourself. An ambulance may cost you $50 to $100 dollars: a lawsuit could cost you your gymnastics career or worse.

Returning to Workout

Usually, if an accident is bad enough that a gymnast must sit out or ice the injury for any period of time, the class for that gymnast should be over. Any gymnast who may be "faking it" to get attention will not make that mistake again. In addition, any gymnast whose injury is more severe than what it seems will be protected. Use your own good judgment. If in doubt, consult with your program director and the gymnast's parents.

The "5 minute rule."

If the gymnast doesn't want to come back within five minutes, or the injury definitely looks and feels worse (increased swelling, bruising, nausea, headache, dizziness, or pain) he is out for the rest of the class or workout.

A gymnast should definitely not return to class if:

1. There is any loss of function (I.E. lack of full range of motion, strength, balance, or sensation.)

2. He is unable to walk / run without limping.

3. Fever or any acute illness is present.

4. There is any sign of dizziness, loss of consciousness (even for a few seconds), memory loss, or tingling in the limbs.

5. He has demonstrated fear due to the injury or accident. This could lead to possible re-injury. You may want to determine if it is the specific skill that causes the fear or the injury itself.

Emergency Action Plan[11]

Develop an emergency action plan among your fellow coaches and instructors so you know what to do when a serious accident occurs in the gym. The coach / instructor with the most knowledge and experience treating injuries should deal with the gymnast in question. Other instructors should take over his / his class and move the other students away from the area and get them involved with other activities to keep their mind off the accident.

Every other instructor should be prepared to adapt to the situation as the need arises. Some instructors may be called on to get First Aid kits, ice, or other necessary items. In an emergency, you may have to call 911. Make sure you stay on the phone and answer all the questions asked by the 911 operator. ***Do not hang up until the 911 operator says it is okay.***

Notify the Parents

No matter how small an injury may seem, it is extremely important that you always notify the parent or guardian when an accident occurs. It may be nothing, but it will go a long way in the public relations department with the gymnast's parents. In addition, if any complication should occur, you have covered yourself much better from a legal standpoint.

---

[11] See Section 15: Miscellaneous Forms for an idea of what is appropriate for an *"Emergency Action Plan"*, and *"Emergency Information Card"* that should be posted by every phone.

Special Note: At the time of the injury you may be feeling emotional and upset over the child's injury. At such a time, it is important that you do not assign guilt to yourself, the gym, anyone, or anything else. When asked about the injury, tell the truth of what happened, for example, "he twisted his ankle doing a back handspring," and let the program director / club owner or the attorneys for the club (if needed) worry about who was at fault. That is what they are paid to do.

If the possibility of fracture or serious injury not requiring a call to 911 is suspected, always suggest to the parents that they see a doctor or go to the emergency room at the hospital.

Keep Records

Always keep a record[12] of every accident that occurs while you are teaching. At the time, it may seem like an insignificant injury, but for any of several reasons it could become a big deal. Whatever the reason, it is doubtful that several weeks later you are going to remember all the particulars about a specific injury.

If your gym does not have an accident report sheet, put one together. Typical information you should report on: the child's full name, age, address, home phone number, note when the parents were contacted, where and when the injury occurred (both gym location and specific piece of equipment), the skill being performed, cause of the accident, steps taken to care for the injured athlete, and statements of any witnesses (and their address and phone numbers).

Keep a copy for your own personal file and always give a copy to the owner or program director of your gymnastics club.

Avoid Dehydration

In warm weather, the gymnast can loose up to 2 quarts of perspiration (sweat) every hour. During hot and humid weather is important to provide water breaks for your students.

---

[12] See sample accident report form in Section 15.

The following is reprinted from the "Gymnastics Safety Guidelines" in the second edition of the *USAG Safety Manual* with permission from the USAG.

Gymnastics Safety Guidelines
SAFETY POSTER I

1. **ASSUMPTION OF RISK.** Participation in gymnastics activities involves motion, rotation, and height in a unique environment and as such carries with it a reasonable assumption of risk.

2. **WARNING!** Catastrophic injury, paralysis, or even death can result from improper conduct of the activity.

3. **POTENTIAL MEDICAL EMERGENCIES.** Instructors/supervisors should be aware of the potential medical emergencies that could occur in gymnastics and be prepared to adequately respond to them in an appropriate manner.

4. **BE PREPARED TO PARTICIPATE.** Dress appropriately, follow accepted warm-up practices, and be mentally prepared to engage in the activity.

5. **CAREFULLY CHECK EQUIPMENT.** Before directly engaging in any gymnastics activity, make sure the equipment is adjusted and secured properly and that adequate matting appropriate to the activity is in the correct position.

6. **CARELESSNESS CANNOT BE TOLERATED.** Gymnastics is an activity requiring active concentration. Horseplay or any other form of carelessness cannot be tolerated at any time for any reason. Consult your instructor.

7. **FOLLOW PROPER SKILL PROGRESSIONS.** A safe learning environment includes a correct understanding of the skill being performed and following proper skill progressions. When in doubt, always consult your instructor.

8. **MASTERING BASIC SKILLS.** Safe learning practices demand mastering basic skills before progressing to new and/or more difficult levels.

9. **ATTEMPTING NEW AND/OR DIFFICULT SKILLS.** The readiness and ability level of the performer, the nature of the task, and the competency of the spotter all must be taken into consideration when attempting a new or difficult skill.

10. **PROPER LANDING TECHNIQUE.** Safe dismounts, as well as unintentional falls, require proper landing techniques. No amount of matting can be a fail-safe. Avoid landing on head or neck at all costs as serious catastrophic injuries may result.

SECTION 5

Spotting

Spotting is the art of maintaining a safe environment for the performance of a gymnastics skill. Using the hands or specialized equipment the instructor will guide a gymnast through the skill during the early learning phases, and for safety, sometimes long after the gymnast has perfected it.

There are three different types of manual spots:

1. The Carry Spot: When a gymnast is first learning a skill and has no idea where to place his hands or for example, when to tuck on a front somersault, it will be your job to step in and physically pick his up and put his through the skill. When you use the carry spot, the gymnast can feel where his body should be and at what time he needs to begin the actions necessary to complete the gymnastics skill successfully.

2. The Control Spot: Once a gymnast has been practicing a skill, but is still unsure of his ability to accomplish the trick safely, you can use the control spot. In this spot, you manipulate the gymnast's body only as much as is necessary for his to complete the skill safely.

3. The Safety Spot: During the safety spot you allow the gymnast to attempt the skill by himself, but stand close enough to spot just in case any assistance is necessary.

Most of the spots just described are done with hand spotting. The instructor uses his hands and the strength of his arms and body to safely catch and/or control the gymnast during the execution of a gymnastics skill.

Your ability to spot will play a large role in how many skills a gymnast is willing to learn, or for that matter even attempt. You only have to drop someone once. After landing in a nose pose a gymnast might say, "Holy cheeseburgers, that hurts!" Convincing the gymnast to go for the skill again may be difficult at this point.

Gymnasts know which instructors are good spotters. They will instinctively shy away from someone they don't feel safe with. The instructor-gymnast relationship has to be very strong and trusting for a gymnast to attempt advanced skills on any of the pieces of gymnastics equipment. The ability to spot gymnastics skills safely is a talent that develops over time with hard work and practice. To develop your spotting abilities attend workshops and clinics. You can also volunteer time with lower level team programs at your gym to learn the art of spotting. Like the gymnast learning the skill, repetition is the key to learning to spot effectively.

When Should I Spot?

(For this section, assume that all areas have matting and/or safety equipment appropriate to the exercise or skill being performed.)

1. If the gymnast has any doubt about his ability to do a skill safely by himself, you should always spot the skill. It is better for you to spot the skill than have a gymnast land on his head.

2. As the instructor you must be sure the gymnast will go for the skill with 100% effort. If you have any doubts, be close enough to spot the gymnast if necessary. To help you decide, answer these questions:

Can the gymnast say in his own words the exact timing and sequence of events that need to take place to successfully complete this skill?
Answer: Evaluate the gymnast's answer.

Is the gymnast strong enough and flexible enough to complete this skill safely?
Answer: The answer should be yes. Did you make that determination from previous testing or just your best guess? Test the gymnast!

How much of a spot have I been giving his to make the skill on previous attempts? A tap or a big lift?
Answer: If you have been consistently decreasing the amount of help you give the gymnast and mostly placing your hand on his body to let his know you are there, he is probably ready to do it himself.

Has the gymnast balked on any previous attempts?
Answer: If a gymnast still balks, chances are there is some part of the skill or instructions that he does not fully understand and the wise instructor will backtrack and go over the skill from the beginning to find out which part is missing.

Usually, after a long relationship the instructor will know when the gymnast is ready to attempt the skill, and on which nights he is not ready and will act accordingly. Some gymnasts are "self starters" and are more than willing to go for a new skill. Other gymnasts may need a little cajoling.

An important point to remember is that when a gymnast goes for a skill 100%, the chance of getting hurt is minimal, much smaller than if he changes his mind in the middle of the skill. That's like trying to change your car from drive to reverse while traveling in a forward direction; all that happens is the gears get stuck somewhere in the middle and the car goes out of control. Basically, the same thing happens when a gymnast changes his mind in the middle of a skill; he loses control, which can lead to injury.

Break it Down

A method the instructor may use for developing a skill, with the minimum of spotting, is to break the skill down into it's basic parts and teach it with the use of mats or other safety devices so the gymnast does most of the skill on his own. If the gymnast is afraid to do a skill without a spot, this method may help his to learn the skill by himself.

To learn more about the basics of gymnastics technique consult the head coach or program director of your gym. An excellent book for basics on gymnastics technique is *"Biomechanics of Women's Gymnastics"* by Dr. Gerald S. George.

Spotting Devices

Many gyms use an overhead spotting belt that may be located over any of the gymnastics apparatus. It consists of a belt that fastens around the gymnast's waist. Ropes connected to either side of the belt extend up to a series of pulleys mounted on support girders in the gym ceiling. The coach holds the other end of the rope and can lift the gymnast in the air keeping his safe while he attempts new skills. This is a specialized device and should be used only by trained and qualified coaches.

In addition to the belt, many gyms have a landing pit. A "pit" is a hole in the ground usually six to eight feet deep, twelve to fifteen feet wide, and twenty to thirty feet long filled to the top with loose foam or specially designed mats.

Gymnasts may practice many different skills, landing in the pit with a high degree of safety, and with less wear and tear on their bodies from hard or slightly out of control landings.

NO LANDING PIT, SAFETY CUSHION, OR SPOTTING DEVICE CAN GUARANTEE A SAFE LANDING!

Landing on the head or stomach as well as several other inappropriate positions can still cause injury in a pit,

If you have been using devices, such as the foam or resi-pit, incline / decline mats, stacks of mats under equipment, or landing mats you must carefully monitor / spot the gymnast as you change the workout conditions to accomplish appropriate skill acquisition.

Caution: Never tell a gymnast you are going to spot if you do not intend to do so. It could cause the gymnast to balk or freeze midway through the skill when the spot is absent, leading to a potentially harmful landing.

Spotting notes:

1. The instructor should spot until the gymnast makes himself familiar with the equipment and workout conditions.

At home in your own gym, this should not be difficult. Later when you take a gymnast to a competition, it will become more important. For any competition, your gymnasts should be able to successfully complete his routines with the skills he will use in that competition at least two weeks before the meet.

2. For difficult skills, a spotter may always need to be standing by just in case.

The reason for this is that when an instructor spots he is, in effect, giving the gymnast a little more air time or support necessary to complete the skill. When the spot is not there, the gymnast may land short, or over rotate the skill and injure himself. A safety spot is always a good idea in this instance.

3. Make every gymnast demonstrate the appropriate progressions and/or drills before you spot them on the "big trick" for the first time. This allows you to evaluate the gymnast's ability level and prepare to spot by first working with them on the lead up skills.

Many young gymnasts like to tell new or substitute instructors; *"I can do that by myself."* Most often, the instructor nearly has a heart attack as the gymnast barely survives the attempt. Always spot if you have any doubts or are unfamiliar with the gymnast.

4. Learn to spot new and/or more difficult skills by double spotting with a coach who is familiar with the skill.

Repetition is the mother of learning so let's go through all the spotting concerns one more time with help from Dr. Gerald George.

SPOTTING - SAFETY FIRST!

The purpose of spotting is to protect the athlete and provide the needed safety assistance to make sure that the chance of injury in performing a new or difficult skill is minimized. The second purpose is to help the athlete accomplish the skill.

Here are ten key safety guidelines that should always be considered in spotting.

1. Be sure that the difficulty level of the skill is appropriate to the capabilities and experiences of the performer.

2. Learn to spot effectively the most basic skills first. Allow sufficient time to adequately master each level spotting progressions.

3. Establish a clear, accurate communication link with the performer.

4. Be absolutely certain that both you and the performer are in the proper position and ready to interact.

5. Be sure you know, understand and appreciate the full potential of the skill, particularly the more critical aspects of how to spot it.

6. Carefully match your own physical readiness and capabilities to that of each individual performer. Always insure that the margin for safety is overwhelmingly in the performer's favor.

7. Learn what to expect from each gymnast. Make every effort to read individual weaknesses.

8. Be prepared for the unexpected. Maintain constant vigilance throughout the skill in its entirety.

9. Develop a healthy respect for the risks and potential hazards involved in any spotting situation. Know your limitations.

10. Always be keenly aware that the prime consideration is protection of the performer's head and spinal column.

- Gerald S. George
USGF Director of Safety [13]

Theory vs. The real world

If you combine the concepts we touched on earlier:

- Strength & Flexibility
- Body Lines / Segmentation
- Center of gravity / Body shapes: mesomorph, ectomorph, endomorph.
- Base of support.
- Lines of force from gravity.
- Vectors of force – horizontal / vertical & angular momentum.
- Pattern of errors: talking less and coaching more.
- Feedback: Senseless cheerleading or positive direction?
- Fear: unconscious body knowledge & its effect on technique;

and apply them when spotting, you will be ahead of the game. If you understand the gymnast lacks the strength to keep his arms next to his ears and his shoulder angle open when attempting a front handspring, your spot will be focused on the gymnast's shoulder, helping to keep it straight throughout the skill attempt.

When your gymnast is attempting skills with rotation, you will use your knowledge of body types and centers of gravity to spot the gymnast near his center of gravity to help with rotation.

An understanding of angular momentum will give you a clue where to go when spotting a round off back handspring. If the gymnast lands the round off with his feet in back of his hips he is either going to block straight up, or he is going to buckle his knees in an attempt to get backward and lose most of the force from the round off through his knees. In any case, he won't be traveling toward you and you will need to be ready to switch gears to go back and get his before he lands in a very painful nose pose.

Finally, there is no substitute for practicing your spotting technique. It will only get better through practice, where you will eventually learn to see patterns of movement in your mind long before you realize that your hand has gone out to automatically spot the gymnast and save his from injury.

---

[13] Publication and date of publication unknown.

SECTION 6

Conditioning

If ever there were a magical technique for obtaining gymnastic skill, it would have to be conditioning. Conditioning is a broad concept, but for the purposes of this chapter, we will focus on two aspects: strength and flexibility.

Strength and flexibility are the two key components most of your gymnasts will require to enable them to do skills with dynamic repulsion, graceful stretch, and artistic poise. Strength and flexibility are also usually the least favorite things a gymnast has to do in class. In addition, for class gymnasts who will be spending only an hour per week, it is not feasible to develop a conditioning program that would take up nearly the whole class. You can, however, develop a strength circuit that takes place on each event while saving flexibility elements for the beginning and ending of class. First, let's start with strength.

Strength

Repulsion from the vault horse, pressing to a handstand, the speed of a vault run, and the ability to hang in an "L" position are all different types of strength that are necessary in gymnastics training.

The importance of strength in gymnastics cannot be over-emphasized. For example, a child incapable of doing a single pull up or leg lift on the bars will be totally frustrated on this event. Unable to lift himself into a basic front support position, he will need to rely on help from the instructor, classmates, or special equipment just to get on the bar. The examples where the need for strength is critical for the achievement of a skill are endless. Unfortunately, there are no magical techniques that can be substituted for a lack of strength, which is why most coaches have strong spotting arms.

Circuit Training

The amount of time you should spend on strength training depends on what type of program you are working with. It is not practical to attempt a strength program during a one-hour gymnastics class unless you create a circuit. For example, a circuit at bars could begin with a hip pullover on a single bar station, then a handstand on a low bar station, and finally a series of push-ups at the last station before the gymnast would start the circuit all over again. The instructor would position himself at the station where the gymnasts need the most help or supervision.

Get The Gymnast's Parents Involved

Plan special weeks where you train both the gymnast and parents. Show them how to do the exercises correctly so they may be practiced at home. It is always advisable to monitor your gymnasts as they practice strength training exercises because they tend to, dare I say it, cheat? When doing the training use the conditioning skills developed for Level 1. The illustrations will show you the proper body positions and list pointers for doing the exercise correctly.

The Level 1 Conditioning program takes into account the exercises most needed by beginner level gymnasts. If you plan to add or subtract from this conditioning program be sure the strength program you develop takes into account each muscle group in the body. Exercising only one half of a muscle group can lead to injury. For example, in the upper arm you have a biceps muscle and triceps muscle. The biceps is most prominent in flexing the upper arm. The triceps on the other hand extends the arm until it is straight. One muscle group works to counteract the activity of the other. In many instances, the opposing muscle acts as a brake to slow down a particular motion.

Can you imagine what would happen if you flexed your arm powerfully with no triceps muscle to slow down your arm at the end of its range of motion? You would probably smack yourself in the mouth. As funny as that might look, the only way you could extend your arm would be to relax your biceps and let gravity cause it to fall. If gravity caused it to fall and you had no biceps to slow down the descent, the result would probably be a dislocated elbow.

The point of the preceding example is to caution you to create a strength circuit that works both the protagonist and antagonistic muscle groups so you do not create a situation where injury can occur.

The purpose of this section is not to train you in exercise physiology, but to make you aware of specific knowledge you need to gain to be a more effective and ultimately safer gymnastic instructor.

Track Your Results

Keep a chart detailing the strength development, or lack of, in each of your gymnasts. It will help determine what the appropriate workout is for each gymnast and when you need to talk to parents about why a child is not prepared to do a new skill or move to the next class level.

CAUTION: Before taking part in any gymnastics activity each participant should have a thorough medical screening or physical. Most school age children have a physical at least once a year. The club application form should have a space for the parent to indicate that his child has had a physical within the past year and is in appropriate physical condition to participate in the sport of gymnastics.

CONDITIONING FOR LEVEL 1
(12 Conditioning Exercises)

- 5 – 20 Sit Ups (Bent Knee)
- 4 – 6 Push Ups (Bent Knee)
- 5 – 6 Arch Ups
- 15 second – Pike Stretch (fingertips on floor)
- Tuck "L" Hang from Low Bar for 2 seconds (tuck position)
- Punch Jumps on floor for 45 seconds.
- 5 semi squat jumps with extension at height of jumps.
- 1 Pull-Up on Single Bar or Chin hold with chin above bar for 5 seconds.
- L-Hold on Single Bar for 5 seconds each.
- 5 – 10 second - Leg lifts-below horizontal (forward, sideward, backward)
- 5 – Inlocates and dislocates (with stick) Hands wide at first, working in closer as flexibility progresses.
- Jog for 1 minute

As you continue your education as a gymnastics instructor, it will be important for you to gain additional information on:

- Anatomy and Kinesiology.
- Breathing techniques during exercise.
- Timing of positive and negative muscle movement.
- Aerobic versus anaerobic training.
- Proper body alignment during the execution of strength training.
- Frequency of training sessions and duration.
- Number of repetitions and sets of each exercise.
- When to increase resistance during an exercise.

Now, let's move on to the other major component in gymnastics conditioning – flexibility.

Flexibility

The ability to move a body part or parts through the broadest range of motion possible, while maintaining strength and stability in the respective joint.

The basics of flexibility are:

1. Get the blood flowing first. Have the gymnasts run a few laps around the floor exercise or do some jumping jacks to get the blood flowing out to the extremities. Microscopic muscle tears may occur when you stretch a "cold" muscle.

2. Perform the stretch in a controlled manner. For our purpose here, there are only two types of stretching: ballistic and static.

Ballistic is a type of stretch where the body is in motion, usually some form of bouncing. Any type of bouncing or flopping into a stretch position can cause tears in the muscle tissue and put undue strain on tendons and ligaments. In addition, the body has what is known as the *stretch reflex*. When you step off a curb and start to twist your ankle, *your* body uses the stretch reflex to snatch your ankle back before it can be injured. If through excess force you overpower this reflex you can tear muscle tissue, strain tendons, or sprain your ankle. You may even cause what is known as an avulsion fracture where the tendon pulls off a piece of bone.

In gymnastics, ballistic stretching is not ideal.

Static stretching occurs when you extend a body part to the end of its normal range of motion and then carefully extend that range until you begin to feel a mild discomfort and then hold that position for thirty seconds to a minute. For the general gymnastics population this is the most appropriate form of stretching.

Off the beaten path

Most young gymnasts tend to take the path of least resistance. Unfortunately, that can mean potential injury. Make sure that each gymnast keeps the body alignment appropriate to the stretch being performed, and isolates and stretches only the specific muscle group according to the respective stretch. Failure to do so could cause the gymnast to stretch the wrong body parts and open his to the possibility of injury.

Design a conditioning program for your class gymnasts that stretches every part of the body as a warm up before class or workout and as a cool down after the class or workout is over. During the class, you can create strength and/or flexibility circuits at each event, making sure to cover each muscle group appropriately.

NOTE: Vary the program content every few months to keep boredom and sloppy performance from becoming normal behavior.

Level 1 Flexibility Skills (see Floor Exercise and Tumbling)
(to be performed after a cardio-warm up)

- Roll out ankles, wrists, neck, and shoulders

- Splits (right & left) 120-140 degrees (30 – 60 seconds each)

- Seated Straddle (Closed position stretching for 30 –60 seconds each to the right leg, left leg, and finally chest to the ground in the center.)

- Seated Pike (Closed position stretching bring the chest to the knees with a flat back and tight knees.)

- Straddle Split 120 degrees (facing the wall, straddle the legs and scoot the hips forward until the legs are out to the sides and the chest and stomach are flat against the wall.

- Bridge (see description under Floor Exercise)

- Shoulder Stand (see description under Floor Exercise)

Photo courtesy of Heather Maynez

SECTION 7

Basic Body Positions

Before going any further the gymnastics instructor should become familiar with the gymnastics terminology that will be used throughout this program. In the Basic Safety Certification program the focus is on the following body positions. The goal in any body position is the least number of lines or body segments appropriate to that position. For example, a seated pike should not have slightly bent knees. In addition, like a balloon, you want to extend or stretch body parts as much as possible. For example, a seated straddle would have arms stretching to the ceiling and toes pointing toward the walls. In all positions the stomach is sucked in and the hips tucked tightly under.

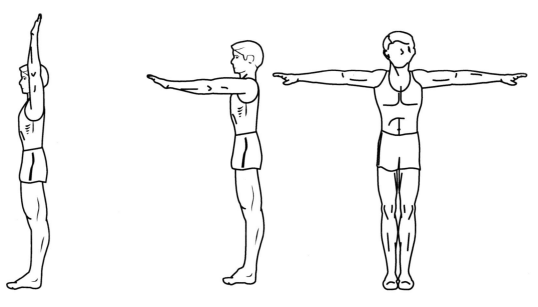

Stretch Position   Attention Position

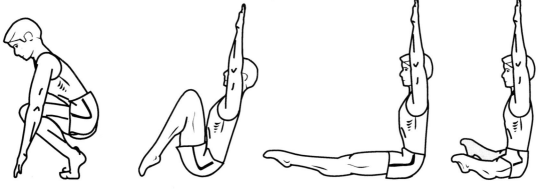

Squat Position   Tuck   Seated Pike (Open)   Seated Straddle (Open)

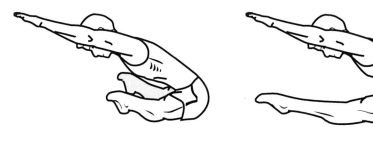

Seated Straddle (Closed)   Seated Pike (Closed)

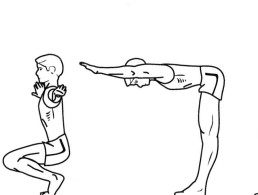

Squat Stand   Standing Pike   Standing Lunge   Standing Straddle

Layout or Supine Position   Prone Position

Rear Support   Front Support

Wolf Stand   Standing Straddle

Olympic Competitive Arena
Photo courtesy of Rita Brown

SECTION 8

Floor Exercise and Tumbling - Overview

If the sport of gymnastics were depicted as a pyramid, then tumbling and floor exercise skills would most certainly and appropriately be the foundation or base. And like a pyramid, the base, or in the instance of gymnastics, the basics are the key elements to build upon and structure a successful and exciting experience in the sport of gymnastics.

Think about it! As an instructor you want to teach a child a front hip circle on the bars. How is that possible without first teaching his the forward rotating movement, a forward roll, on the floor? The same is true for each of the other events. To do a front handspring on vault, the gymnast must have attained some measure of skill in practicing the handstand on floor. Isn't beam simply the perfection of floor exercise and tumbling skills? Think about it, forward rolls, cartwheels, handstands, all on a four-inch wide surface, raised off of the floor to varying heights. If the gymnast has not perfected the skill on floor, he certainly will not make it on the beam!

Of all the events, floor will, initially, be the most important. The gymnast will learn the correct terminology for body positions and skill names. The gymnast will learn how to do the "core" or basic skills: the handstand, forward roll, backward roll, the cartwheel, and physical conditioning (strength & flexibility). The origin of most gymnastics skills can be traced back to these basic skills. The head is the heaviest part of the body and when the chin is dropped to the chest, the body will tend to pike. When the head is tilted backward, the body tends to arch. The position of the head is very important and will affect the outcome or landing positions of all gymnastics skills.

As an instructor in the Level 1 Certification program you have been charged with an awesome responsibility; the training of correct basic skills. In essence, you are the most important coach the gymnast will ever have. You set the standard and the technique. If a gymnast has talent and eventually makes it to higher levels or even a team program, the coach will have to regress the gymnast for any sloppy or incorrect basic techniques. Your diligence in training correct basics will enable each of your gymnasts to progress smoothly and attain a higher degree of success.

Remember, the basics for the basics begins with the least number of body segments necessary for the skill, appropriate body line and muscular tension to maintain form and perform the skill with adequate range of motion or flexibility, and strength related such as explosive punch for powerful tumbling and amplitude.

Finally, it is not what the gymnast does, but how he does it (with form) that will cause your gymnasts to stand out and excel.

Level 1 Floor and Tumbling begins on the next page.

Floor Exercise & Tumbling Level 1

Floor Level 1 contains all the elements the gymnast will need to be successful on all the gymnastics apparatus. Each of the other events has it's main focus; vault = run, beam = balance, bars = swing, but floor has them all in the one event. Floor is the basic for all the other events. To learn a front hip circle on bars the gymnast must first learn forward rotation on floor via the forward roll. To do a handspring vault the gymnast must first master the handstand on the floor. Level 1 Floor introduces the beginner gymnast to all the basic body positions, dance elements, and the key floor skills. It is vitally important that each gymnast learn the terminology associated with each body position as the instructor will use the positions as the basis for teaching all floor elements. Always use the most appropriate mat or skill cushions when introducing a new tumbling skill.

Floor Exercise Body Positions

Prone Position
The gymnast lays flat on his stomach on the floor with arms extended above his head and tight next to his ears. Stomach should be sucked in and lower back rounded with the seat tight. Arms and legs press down against the floor.

Supine position (layout)

The gymnast lays on his back on the floor with arms extended above his head and tight next to the his ears. Stomach should be sucked in and lower back rounded with the seat tight. Arms and legs press down against the floor.

Front support

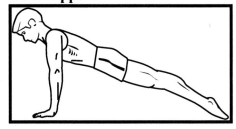

From a prone position on the floor, have the gymnast bend his arms and place the palms of his hands flat on the floor in line with his shoulders and then push up until the arms are straight. From head to toe, the body should be tight, stomach sucked in, lower back rounded, and seat tight.

Rear support

From a "seated pike position" (open), have the gymnast place both hands on the floor directly beside his hips and then push down with the arms while at the same time pressing down with the heels and extend the hips until the body is in a straight line from head to toes. Keep the stomach in, lower back rounded, and seat tight.

Squat stand

From a "squat" position, have the gymnast lift the chest upright and lift the arms to side-middle position. The student should maintain good posture with seat over heals and shoulders inline directly over the heals.

Standing Straddle

From a "stretch" position have the gymnast place his feet slightly wider than his shoulder width on the floor while keeping his arms extended above his head and next to his ears. Maintain body tightness.

Pike stand

From a "stretch" position, while keeping the arms extended above the head and next to the ears, have the gymnast bend at the waist until a 90 degree angle is created between the upper body and the gymnast's legs.

Attention
Standing on the floor, have the gymnast suck in the stomach, round his lower back, and squeeze his seat. The arms are tight against the sides of the body with fingers pointing down the leg. Head is in neutral position. Maintain body tightness.

Forward lunge position
From a "stretch" position, while keeping the arms extended above the head and next to the ears, have the gymnast take a step forward and finish with the front knee bent to a 45-degree angle. The back leg should remain straight. Toes should be pointed.

Wolf stand
From a "stretch" position, while keeping the arms extended above the head and next to the ears, have the gymnast take a step to one side and completely bend the knee until the back of the thigh is resting upon the heel. At the same time, the gymnast lowers his arms to side-middle position.

Stretch position
Standing on the floor, have the gymnast suck in the stomach, round his lower back, and squeeze his seat. The arms are also raised above the head and tight to the ears with fingers extended. Head is in neutral position. Maintain body tightness.

Balance on toes (5 sec.)
From a stretch position, have the gymnast rise up on his toes and maintain balance for at least 5 seconds. The arms are raised above the head and tight to the ears with fingers extended. Head is in neutral position. Maintain body tightness.

Tuck sit
From a "seated pike – open," have the gymnast tuck the knees to the chest.

Star
Starting from stretch position, have the gymnast lower his arms to the 10:00 and 2:00 o'clock positions. Then, have the gymnast separate his legs to the 8:00 and 4:00 position so that in conjunction with the head the body creates a "star" position.

Seated Straddle (open position)
Have the gymnast sit on the floor and extend both feet in front of his and parted approximately twice shoulder width. The chest should be upright with the arms extended above the head and tight to the gymnast's ears. Head is in neutral position. Maintain body tightness with stomach sucked in and lower back slightly rounded.

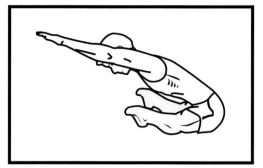

Seated Straddle (closed position)
Start from "seated straddle – open" position and lower the chest to the floor keeping the back flat and arms extended with fingers reaching forward as far as possible.

Seated Pike (open position)
Have the gymnast sit on the floor and extend both feet in front of his squeezed tightly together with the toes pointed. The chest should be upright with the arms extended above the head and tight to the gymnast's ears. Head is in neutral position. Maintain body tightness with stomach sucked in and lower back slightly rounded.

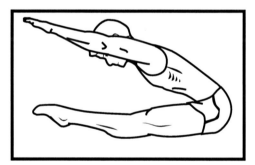

Seated Pike (closed position)
Start from "seated pike – open" position and lower the chest to the legs keeping the back flat and arms extended with the fingers reaching past the toes.

Squat
Standing on the floor at attention, have the gymnast bend his knees and place his hands flat on the floor next to his feet or just to the sides of his toes.

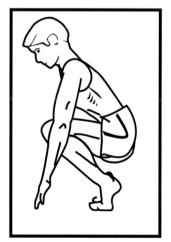

1. Splits (right) – 120 to140 degrees.

The gymnast starts in a kneeling position and extends one leg in front, slowly extending the leg forward along the floor in front of the body. The gymnast must keep the hips square, the back knee turned under, and slowly relax the muscles on the back of the front leg and the front of the back leg. Do not bounce to achieve this position! Initially, the hands may be placed on either side of the body for balance and then gradually lifted above the head and tight to the ears. Switch legs and repeat.

2. Splits (left) – 120 to 140 degrees
Same as Splits (right), but switch legs and repeat.

3. Straddle split – 120 degrees

From a "seated straddle" position have the gymnast continue to widen the straddle focusing on knees up and tight with toes pointed. Starting with heels on a line on the floor and then scooting the hips forward will help to indicate the degree of split. The gymnast's arms are up above the head and tight to the ears.

4. Bridge

From a "layout" position on the floor, the gymnast bends his knees

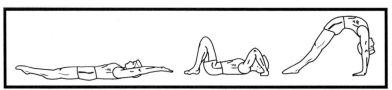

until his feet are flat on the floor. The gymnast's hands are then placed flat on the floor next to his ears. From this position, the gymnast straightens the arms and legs lifting the hips off the floor until the back and shoulders attain a graceful arched position. Keep the head in between the arms, the gymnast may look between his eyebrows to spot his hands on the floor. The legs should be as straight as possible depending on each individual's flexibility.

Note: Have the gymnast work toward stretching his shoulders directly over or slightly forward of the hands. A gentle rock in the shoulders will work flexibility in this area. Spot the upper back and shoulders and emphasize good form as shown in the illustration above.

5. Shoulder stand

From a layout position on the floor, have the gymnast bring both arms down and to his sides with palms pressing flat on the floor. Next, tuck the knees up to the chest and then extend the legs straight in the air creating a ninety-degree angle between the body and the arms, which control the balance by pressing against the floor.

6. Swedish Fall

From a stretch position on the floor, the gymnast lifts one leg into a scale position while also lowering the arms until they are directly in front of the shoulders. From this position, the gymnast does a controlled fall to a landing cushion bending the elbows to carefully absorb the force of the fall. The extended leg remains in a raised position throughout the fall.

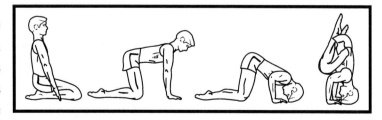

7. Knee scale

From a kneeling position on the floor, the gymnast should reach forward and place both hands on the floor directly beneath his shoulders, and then lift either the right or left leg upward-backward until it is fully extended above the hips in a scale.

8. Tripod

From a kneeling position on the floor, the gymnast should reach forward and place both hands on the floor directly beneath his shoulders, and then slowly place his head on the floor (creating an equilateral triangle with the hands and head). Next, the gymnast places one knee, then the other on the respective elbows to complete the tripod.

Note: Spot from the back side and help balance legs on elbows.

9. Tucked headstand
Starting from a tripod position on the floor, slowly lift the knees from the elbows until a ninety-degree angle is created at the hip joint.

Note: Spot from back side guiding legs slowly upward.

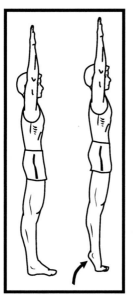

10. Relevé Stand
From a "stretch" position on the floor, the gymnast raises up onto the balls of his feet. Maintain body tightness with head in neutral position.

11. Two foot releve` ½ turn
From a stretch position on the floor, the gymnast rises onto the balls of his feet and pivots 180 degrees. Maintain body tightness with head in neutral position.

12. Scale (low back leg)

From a stretch position on the floor, keeping the leg extended and tight, the gymnast lifts either the left or right leg until the toes of the extended leg are on a line with the back of the support leg knee.

13. Forward Passé` stand (Stork stand)
From a stretch position on the floor, the gymnast lifts one knee until the toes from the lifted leg touch the bottom of the knee on the support leg.

14. Squat ½ turn

From a squat position on the floor, the gymnast lifts his arms above his head, and then using the head to initiate the turn, pivot on the balls of both feet to complete a half turn.

15. Handstand against the wall

From a stretch position on the floor, in front of a stable padded wall, have the gymnast step through lunge position and maintaining arms above the head and tight to the ears, kick up to a handstand using the wall to maintain balance. Stomach should be sucked in, lower back rounded, and seat tucked under. The head should remain in neutral.

Note: Spot from the side adding with control and balance position.

16. Prone fall from knees

From a kneeling position on the floor with the arms extended above the head, the gymnast lowers the arms until they are extended directly forward from his shoulders, and then he falls forward to catch the floor by bending the elbows and lowering the body slowly to the floor.

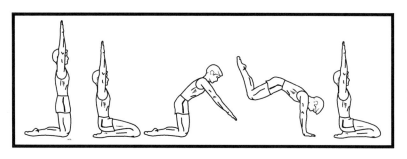

17. Cast hips up from knees

From a kneeling position on the floor with arms extended above the head, have the gymnast sit back until his seat touches his heels. Next, have the gymnast reach forward quickly with both arms and place them on the floor under the shoulders. Let the momentum of the arm reach carry through during the push off through the knees, which help to lift the hip and heels above the shoulders. Lower slowly back to the start position.

18. Front support to rear support

From a prone position on the floor, the gymnast places both hands next to the shoulder and raises the body into a push up position. From this position, the gymnast shifts his weight to one arm while quickly reaching up, in back, and then behind his to finish with both arms holding the body supported with the hips fully extended off the ground. Maintain body tightness with head in neutral position.

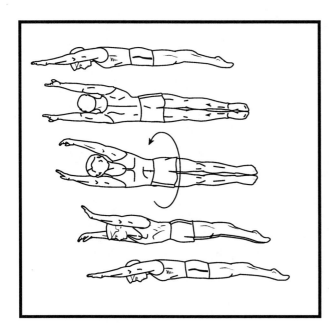

19. Log rolls
From a layout position on the floor, keeping the bodyline straight and tight initiate a roll to the right or left.

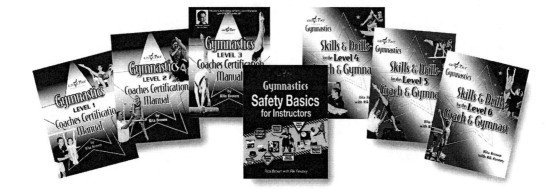

Photo Courtesy of Heather Maynez

20. Ballet positions

1st, 2nd, 3rd, 4th, 5th positions (from left to right 1 to 5)

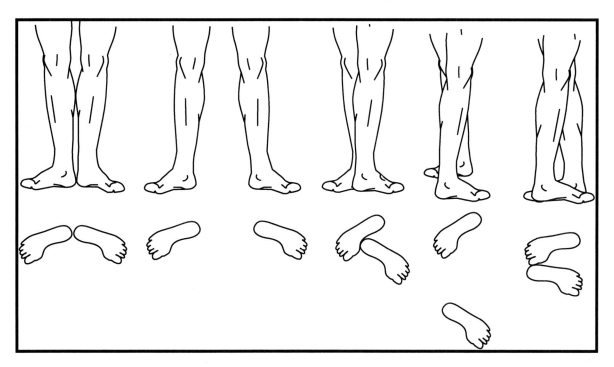

1st position: the balls of both feet are turned out; the heels touch and form a single straight

2nd position: right and left feet approximately 10 inches apart with the toes pointing to 4:00 and 8:00 respectively.

3rd position: one foot is in front of the other, the heel of each foot touching the middle of the other foot. Ex. left foot – toes pointing to approximately 3:30, right foot – heel to the instep of the left foot with toes pointing to 9:00.

4th position: the toe of one foot is directly in front of the heel of the other, the feet are parallel and one short step apart. Ex. right foot – turned out to the 7:00 position, left foot – heal to the big toe of the right foot and toes pointing to 4:00.

5th position: both feet touch so that the toe of one foot reaches the heel of the other foot. Ex. right foot – forward with toes pointing to 9:00, left foot – little toe to heel of right foot with toes pointing to 3:30.

21. Assemble`

From an attention position on the floor, the gymnast steps forward and kicks one extended leg forward / upward, and then closes the bottom leg to the top leg at the peak of the jump. The gymnast lands with both knees slightly bent on the floor. Maintain body tightness with head in neutral.

23. Stretch jump (punch jumps)

From a stretch position on the floor, the gymnast bends his knees and explosively straightens the body to jump as high as possible. Emphasize good body position throughout.

24. V-sit

From a tuck position on the floor, the gymnast lowers his arms to side-middle while extending the knees from tuck to a straight position leaving the gymnast to balance on his hips/seat.

25. Tip up (two point balance)
From a kneeling position on the floor, the gymnast places both hands shoulder-width apart on the floor, and then slowly places both his knees onto his elbows and balances in this position. Spot at the hips for balance.

26. Tripod to tucked headstand to headstand (3 seconds)
From a kneeling position on the floor, the gymnast should reach forward and place both hands on the floor directly beneath his shoulders, and then slowly place his head on the floor (creating an equilateral triangle with the hands and head.) Next, the gymnast places one knee, then the other on the respective elbows to complete the tripod. Next, slowly lift the knees from the elbows until a ninety-degree angle is created at the hip joint. Finally, extend the legs straight up into a headstand position and hold for three seconds. Spot the back and the legs for balance and control through out the skill.

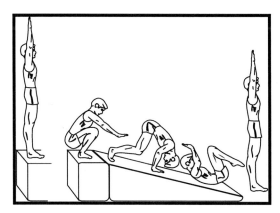

27. Tuck forward roll down incline
From a stretch position, the gymnast reaches down into a squat position on an incline mat and tucks his head under to roll through a tuck position back to a stand in stretch position. Have the gymnast reach forward as he stands up.

28. Tuck forward roll to squat stand
From stretch position on the floor, the gymnast reaches down into a squat position and tucks his head under to roll through a tuck position back to a stand in stretch position.

29. Tuck forward roll to straddle sit

From stretch position on the floor, the gymnast reaches down into a squat position and tucks his head under to roll through a straddle position to finish in a seated straddle.

30. Tuck forward roll to a straddle stand

From stretch position on the floor, the gymnast reaches down into a squat position and tucks his head under to roll through a straddle position back to a standing straddle position. Aid from behind by assisting the straddle stand up position with support to the hips.

31. Lead up to a cartwheel

Place a folded panel mat or small spotting block up against a padded wall. Have the gymnast stand in stretch position with his back almost brushing the wall. Next, the gymnast reaches sideways / downward to place both hands on the block while pushing off the front leg to kick through a side handstand position with back still brushing the wall, to finally step down and finish standing in a stretch position with back against the wall.

32. Cartwheel

Standing with back to a wall (padded) and starting in stretched position, the gymnast reaches sideways / downward to place the hands on the floor in a handstand position and then continues to rotate laterally and step down one leg at a time to finish facing in the same direction as the starting a standing straddle position. Be sure to use an equal rhythm: hand-hand, foot-foot, when practicing this skill.

33. Backward roll to straddle stand – down incline

From a standing straddle position on an incline mat, the gymnast bends forward to place both hands between his feet on the mat, and then slightly bends his knees to allow the hips to lower carefully to the mat, where the gymnast will then straighten his legs and push with both hands (placed next to his ears) until he finishes in a standing straddle.

34. Tuck backward roll to sit on heels

From a stretch position on the floor, the gymnast squats down and backward to continue into a tucked backward roll, which finishes with the gymnast on his knees with his seat touching his heels. Focus on a strong push with the arms to prevent strain on the gymnast's neck.

Note:
Spot by lifting the hips up and over the head.

35. Tuck backward roll from feet to feet

From a stretch position on the floor, the gymnast squats down and backward to continue into a tucked backward roll, which finishes in a stretch position. Focus on a strong push with the arms to prevent strain on the gymnast's neck.

Note: Spot by lifting the hips up and over the head with control and balance.

SECTION 9

Vault- Overview

Vaulting is essentially another form of tumbling. The key to the vault is a consistent powerful run with a smooth transition (hurdle) onto the springboard, where the punch off from the board launches the body toward the horse (mats). When the body approaches the horse at the proper angle the gymnast must be capable of rebounding through the hands, shoulders, and chest with a tight body so he will spring from the horse (mats) into a stretched body position and sail to a graceful landing. The basic parts of a vault are the run, the hurdle, the punch off the board, the pre-flight, the repulsion from the horse, the after-flight, and the landing.

The Level 1 Certification program for Vault focuses on the most important part of vault, which is the run, hurdle, and punch off the board.

Many coaches get caught up in training what happens after the gymnast hits the horse; mainly the repulsion and the after flight, which is where the actual "trick" takes place. The run and hurdle on vault can be compared to the run, hurdle, back handspring before the back somersault on floor. If there is no power in the hurdle, round off back handspring; how high will the somersault be? The answer is not very high. The same is true on vault. If the gymnast does not have a fast run with a low hurdle to transfer the speed of the run to the board quickly, he will not get much power or bounce from the board. No bounce or power from the board means a poor vault.

How far the board is set from the horse (in Level 1; mats) is determined by the speed of the run and the punch from the board. The faster the gymnast runs and the stronger and tighter his bounce, the farther away from the horse or mats the board needs to be to enable the gymnast to fully extend his shoulder angle and stretch his body before contact with the horse or the mats. Note: To help prevent stutter-stepping before the hurdle, have the gymnast focus on the board only during his run.

Level 1 Vault certification focuses on a series of drills to create proper run, hurdle, and board techniques. Level 1 Vault begins on the next page.

Vault – Level 1

Vault

In Vault Level 1, the gymnast is introduced to a dynamic, explosive, and exhilarating event. If you look away, you just might miss the fast run, the quick bounce, and the tight body soaring through the air to punch off the horse; execute the vault and stick a perfect landing.

Fast Run / Quick Bounce / Tight Body; those are the keys to vaulting and the core elements of the Level 1 Vault program. The gymnast focuses on correct arm movement synchronized with effective running skills that lead into a powerful hurdle and tight body punch off the springboard. In this section it is important for the gymnast to correct errors in running technique, develop a focus on the springboard during the run, continuously accelerate toward the board and maintain body tightness to transfer power from the run into the preflight portion of the vaulting skill.

1. Safety Landing Position
Before teaching the gymnast to run and rebound off a springboard or any other gymnastics apparatus, he should be taught the proper method for landing from any vault skill safely. To practice the "safety landing position" the gymnast must always land feet first with his knees slightly bent, his lower back rounded, and his arms raised up between shoulder and head height.

2. Arm & Leg Synchronization – Marching

Just like a toy soldier the gymnast marches down the vault runway focusing on exaggerated steps with high knee lift with opposing arm lift (I.E. left knee lifted with right arm lifted, right knee lifted with left arm lifted)

3. Skipping
With arms and legs in opposition, have the gymnast practice skipping up and down the vault runway.

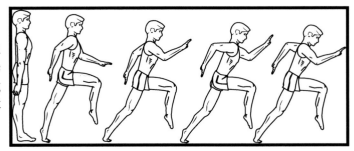

4. Step hurdle – no board.

From a stand, have the gymnast take one step forward and then land with two feet together. The step should be long and low. **Not** high in the air with knee up like in a diving board approach.

5. Step hurdle with backward arm circle – no board.

From a stand, have the gymnast take one step forward while lifting the arms forward and upward. As the gymnast continues forward to land on two feet, the arms continue circling backward and down to finish at the sides of the body. Note: Hurdle step is long and low.

6. Run – no board

Using the vault runway, the gymnast focuses on correct arm and leg usage. Focus on the knees lifting directly in front of the body, and on each step through lifting the heel almost as high as the seat before pulling the leg through again. The arms should be bent at 90 – 120 degrees and pump back and forth with the fist rising to chest level on each swing forward. As in skipping the arms and legs should be in opposition.

7. Stretch jump over objects

The gymnast starts at attention and jumps up and over a foam block, circling the arms backward and down to land and then immediately repeats the process over several other objects. This drill focuses on arm circle and explosive stretch open of the shoulders on each jump.

8. Punch jumps on springboard in front of horse or mat or with spotter.

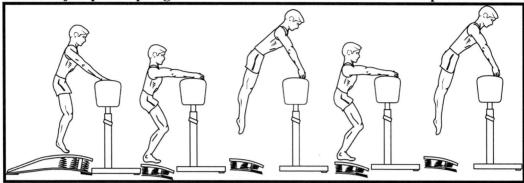

Tight legs on the springboard are key to effective vaulting. To practice, have the gymnast stand on the springboard, which is arm's length from the horse, and practice punching the board ten times in a row with tight legs. This drill may also be done with the instructor holding the gymnast's hands. Emphasize quick punches to the board.

9. Jump from springboard (no run)

From a stand on the springboard, arms down and slightly back of the body, the gymnast bends the knees and jumps while swinging the arms up to a stretched position and then lands in a stop bounce / safety landing position on the mat.

10. From panel mat, jump to springboard with arm circle; rebound.

Standing on a panel mat, the gymnast takes a one or two-step hurdle to a two foot landing then rebound from a springboard. On the last step before the hurdle, the gymnast's arms should rise forward / upward and  as he comes to a landing on the board circle backward / down to finish at the gymnast's sides as the feet contact the board. Landing from the stretch jump should be in a stop bounce / safety landing position. This is an excellent drill for Level 1 gymnasts.

11. Punch jumps on springboard in front of horse or mat with spotter.

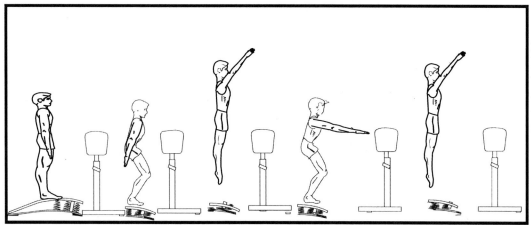

Tight legs on the springboard is key to effective vaulting. To practice, have the gymnast stand on the springboard, which is arm's length from the horse, and practice punching the board ten times in a row with tight legs. This drill may also be done with the instructor holding the gymnast's hands.

Safety landing drills should be reviewed
before the remaining skills.

12. Run, hurdle, punch board, stretch jump to safety landing.
[From springboard to 8-inch landing cushion.] The gymnast should do a half-speed run using good arm and leg synchronization to a hurdle with a backward arm circle, and then land with tight legs on the board to punch off into a stretch body position and finish in a safety landing position on the 8-inch cushion. Speed of the run may be increased as the gymnast demonstrates more proficiency.

13, 15, 16, 17.   Run, hurdle, punch board, to tuck jump [then straddle, then pike, then ½ turn, then 1/1 turn.

Follow the directions from "run, hurdle, punch board, stretch jump," substitute the "stretch jump" for a "tuck jump", and so on. Always have the gymnast finish in a safety landing position on the 8-inch cushion. Speed of the run may be increased as the gymnast demonstrates more proficiency.

* Emphasize control and spot the landing of the ½ turn and 1/1 turn landings.

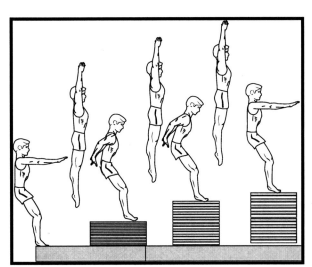

14. Stretch jump up levels

The gymnast starts at attention, and then bends the knees and jumps up, while explosively stretching the arms overhead, to land on the next block from which he immediately jumps to the next higher block and sticks the landing. Spot from the side or in front of the block.

18. Squat Thrusts

From a front leaning support on the floor, shift the weight to the hands and bring the knees forward to a squat position. Then return to a front leaning support and repeat the activity 3-5 times. This drill would be a good conditioning exercise for level 1.

19. Bounces to squat on, jump off

From a stand on the springboard with hands on top of the mats bounce 3-5 times and squat onto the mats. Immediately jump off the mats and land in safety landing position; rise to stand. Spot from the side following gymnast to controlled landing position.

USA Coaches Certification, Inc.

20. Squat on, jump off (from walk)

Walk forward 3-5 steps, hurdle, and rebound off the board with two feet. Vault to a squat position on the mats, immediately jump forward off the mats and land in safety landing position; rise to stand. Spot from the side to a controlled landing position.

21. Squat on, jump off (from run)

Run 3-5 steps, hurdle, and rebound off the board with two feet. Vault to a squat position on the mats, immediately jump forward off the mats and land in safety landing position; rise to stand. Spot from the side to a controlled landing position.

22. Squat Vault

Run3-5 steps, hurdle, and rebound off the springboard with two feet. Reach forward with arms to a front support and simultaneously push off the mat with both hands and tuck the knees. After passing over the mats, extend the legs to land in safety landing position; rise to stand. Spot from the side to a controlled landing position.

23. Run, hurdle, punch jump – forward roll

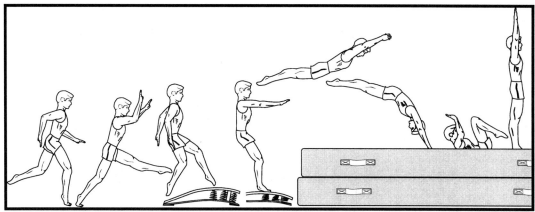

From one or two steps, hurdle, and rebound off the board landing execute a forward roll to stand. Emphasize control and tight body throughout. Spot from the side and guide the weight of the gymnast onto the landing mat. Keeping most of the weight off the mat until the gymnast safely tucks his head under and begins to roll out.

24. Traveling jumps – up and down the folded mat

With folded panel mats set end-to-end, travel forward with support on the hands by jumping from the side of the mat to the top of the mat, to the other side of the mat, back to the top, and so forth. Each time the feet have support on the floor move the hand forward 6"-12".

USA Coaches Certification, Inc.

SECTION 10

High Bar – Horizontal Bar – Pipe – Single Bar: Overview

The men's high bar is one of three events that contain the element of swing. Other pieces of equipment may use partial swing or parts of the body may swing through various skills but the high bar, rings and parallel bars are the events that the whole body must swing completely around the apparatus.

The Level 1 Certification program for Bars focuses on basic handgrip positions, basic swings, supports, circling moves, and introductory level dismounts. The most important thing all these skills have in common is that the hands of the young gymnast's are going to get mighty hot and blistered the first few times they work on the bars.

A little preparation and TLC will go a long way, when a gymnast comes to you with a blister or a rip. Blisters and rips are common and occur frequently with novice gymnasts as their hands adapt to the changes and forces that occur when performing various swing movements on the bar. Part of the reason is the lack of understanding on how to shift their grip properly during the swing action. Some gymnasts grip the bar to hard creating excessive friction on the hands know to many coaches as a "death-grip." The gymnast holds the bar so tight he causes blisters to form quickly. The cure is to practice grip shifting drills right away, teach the kids to soak their hands in cool water after class, and then use hand lotion to keep them moist.

Grips

Grips are an excellent way of reducing the amount of friction on the hand when performing swing movements on the high bar. Gymcert recommends you consult with your experienced coach/instructor when considering this option. Grips are inexpensive and can be found on most gymnastics apparel web sites or proshops. Dowel grips and not recommended for the novice bar worker. Dowel grips are intended for upper level skills.

The other important consideration for bars is upper body and abdominal strength. Many young gymnasts are sadly lacking in this area. Add upper body and abdominal drills to the circuit program on bars. In addition, always use at least an eight-inch landing cushion under the bar, as well as other panel mats and shaped mats to create a mechanical advantage for the gymnast to complete the skill on his own.

The Level 1 Boy's Certification program for Bars begins on the next page.

Men's Horizontal Bar – Level 1

Gymnasts should be made familiar with the three basic grips used for bar work. The instructor should demonstrate each of these grips with skills using the low bar or single bar.

| **Over Grip** | **Reverse Grip** | **Mix Grip** |

Thumbs always around the bar.

1. Single Bar Grips
Over Grip (far left picture)

The "Over Grip" is the most commonly used grip on the high bar. If using a women's rail, the gymnast should keep the thumb and fingers together unless using the thumb as a "brake" to slow down a circling skill. **Remember**: Anytime the body is rising it is virtually weightless and is the appropriate time for the gymnast to shift or re-establish his grip on the bar.

Note: Hand guards (or grips) may not be appropriate for the young gymnast until he can effectively shift his grip on backward – upward swings and circling swings around the bar.

Reverse Grip (middle picture)

The thumbs and fingers are around the bar with the palms facing toward the gymnast and the thumbs on the outside around the bar.

Mix Grip (far right picture)

The "Mix Grip" is a combination of the Over grip and the Reverse grip being used at the same time. Typically, this grip is used when the gymnast wants to complete a half turn during a swing.

Single Bar Body Positions
Introduce and demonstrate each body position so the gymnast is prepared for working these skills on a low bar.

The key to effective bar work is body extension at all times. When in a support position, the gymnast should not relax and let the stomach help to hold him on the bar. The gymnast should push down on the bar until the arms are fully extended and the bar rests lightly on the thighs. There are relatively few times when the gymnast actually pulls in to the bar. In most instances, it is important that the gymnast maintain full extension of the arms and legs through each skill attempt.

Note: the area under the bar should have at least a basic mat (1 ¼ inch) and a landing mat (4 inches) or preferably a landing mat (4 inches) and a safety-landing cushion (8 inches).

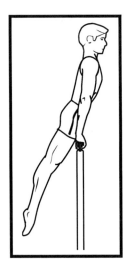

2. Front support – low bar

Using one or two panel mats under the bar as a platform, the gymnast places both hands on the bar. Keeping the arms straight, the gymnast bends his knees slightly and jumps to a support with the arms on the bar. The bar should cross the top of the gymnast's thighs. It is important to maintain tight arms (no resting on the belly!) with the body in a slight, tight arch. Head should remain in neutral. Spot the arms and shoulders for balance and control.

3. Rear support – low bar

Sufficient panel mats should be placed under the bar that will allow the gymnast to literally sit down backwards on the bar with both hands at the sides. The gymnast then lifts his extended legs off the mat to a balance position with the bar crossing just under his seat.

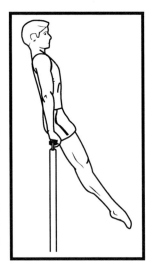

Note: The instructor should spot or provide sufficient matting and safety landing instruction should the gymnast lose balance and fall backward. This skill should be spotted from the backside giving support to the back.

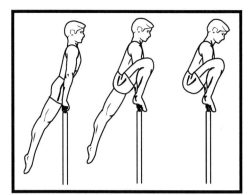

4. Climb to perch stand – low bar – 5 seconds

Preparation: Using a portable resi-pit or a stack of landing cushions build a platform of mats in front of the bar that comes to within 12 inches of the height of the bar. In addition, use one or two panel mats under the bar as a mounting platform.

From a front support position on the low bar, the gymnast carefully climbs up one leg at a time to finish with the right foot outside the right hand on the bar, and the left foot outside the left hand on the bar in a squat position. Hold for 5 seconds. Spot from the front of the bars spotting the gymnasts shoulders and arms for correct balance.

5. Skin the cat to hang and back again to long hang position

Note: To prevent shoulder injury, this skill should first be practiced on a low bar that will allow the gymnast to touch his feet to the floor at the ending phase of the skill.

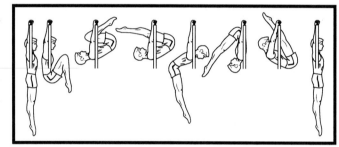

From a stand in front of the low bar, the gymnast grasps the bar in a shoulder-width "over grip." Next, the gymnast pulls both knees up to the chest and continues to tuck up until he can extend his legs through his arms and continue to extend the legs down to the floor. The gymnast can push off the floor slightly to help his pull through his shoulders and reverse the direction of movement back to the starting position. When proficient, the gymnast can move to a higher bar. Spot from the side guiding the legs through the arms and hold onto one wrist for safety and support.

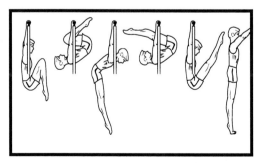

6. Pike inverted hang

Preparation: There must be a minimum of a 4-inch landing mat and an 8-inch landing cushion under the low bar for this skill.

From a stand in front of the low bar, the gymnast grasps the bar in a shoulder-width "over grip." Next, the gymnast pulls both knees up to the chest and continues to tuck up until he can extend his legs through his arms past the bar to an extended position with his back and legs parallel to the floor. Spot from side and hold onto one wrist while the other hand aids the gymnast throughout the skill.

7. Straight body inverted hang

Preparation: There must be a minimum of a 4-inch landing mat and an 8-inch landing cushion under the low bar for this skill.

From a stand in front of the low bar, the gymnast grasps the bar in a shoulder-width "over grip." Next, the gymnast pulls both knees up to the chest and continues to tuck up until he can extend his legs through his arms and continue to extend the legs with toes pointed to the ceiling until they are straight with hips extended and the seat rests against the low bar. Maintain body tightness with the head in neutral position. Spot from the front side of the bars by lifting legs upward for support and guiding through out the skill. Watch the hands for gripping and control. One hand can hold the wrist for additional support while the other hand guides the legs.

8. Single knee hang

From a stand in front of the low bar, the gymnast grasps the bar in a shoulder-width "over grip." Next, the gymnast pulls both knees up to the chest and tucks one leg through. The gymnast's leg extends over the low bar and bends at the knee so the bar crosses at the back of the knee. Spot the upper back with one hand and the straight leg with the other.

9. Glide hang

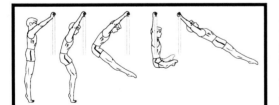

From a stand in front of a lower bar, the gymnast grasps the bar in a shoulder-width "over grip." Next, the gymnast pushes off the floor from a slight knee bend and lifts the legs into a seated straddle position as he swings back and forth.

Note: Stand behind the gymnast to aid in the lift of the hips during the extension after the knee bend. Avoid the legs when straddling into the glide. If you spot the front side of the extension you can assist the legs coming together at the end of the glide to help in attaining full extension.

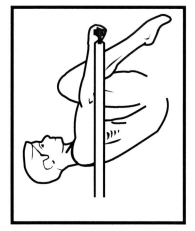

10. Tuck inverted hang

From a stand in front of the low bar, the gymnast grasps the bar in a shoulder-width "over grip." Next, the gymnast pulls both knees up to the chest and continues to tuck up until he can touch his knees to his nose and his heels to his seat in a tight tucked position. Spot the wrist of the gymnast with one hand while guiding his legs up then support should be given to his rounded back. Watch the gymnast's hands for grip control. Very young children may just let go for no reason. Be ready!

11. Grip walks

Hanging from the bar in a shoulder-width "over grip," the gymnast slides the left hand down the bar six to twelve inches, and then slides the right hand a similar distance to return to the shoulder-width over grip. This process is repeated until the gymnast has traversed the length of the low bar.

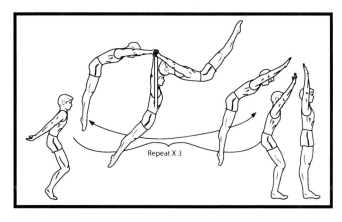

Repeat X 3

12. Long Hang Swings

Preparation: Raise the bar to a height relevant to the level and size of the gymnasts. Most gymnasts will be able to hang underneath, even with an 8-inch landing cushion underneath and not be able to touch their toes.

The gymnast jumps up to the low bar in a shoulder-width over grip and by learning to alternately arch, then hollow begins to "pump" a controlled long hang swing. Initially, it may be best for the gymnast to learn to swing out of the wrist rather than re-adjusting the grip at the peak of each back swing. The gymnast finishes the swing by letting go of the bar at the peak of the backward swing and landing with knees slightly bent, lower back rounded, and arms next to the ears. Spot from the backside with hand on back of gymnast and one hand on his wrist. Follow through and guide to the finish landing position. Review proper landing procedures and release timing before teaching this skill.

13. Forward roll on low bar to stand

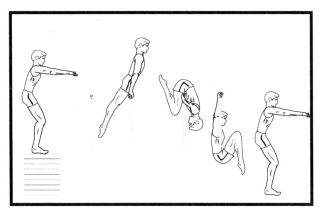

The gymnast jumps to a front support position from a panel mat and continues his rotation forward by sliding his grip around the bar and tucking his knees to roll over the bar to a stand. Spot the jump up onto the bar from behind the gymnast by lifting the hips or waist. Guide the roll down with one hand on the back and one hand on the tucked legs for control and smoothness.

14. 3 cast preparations (hips on bar) – low bar

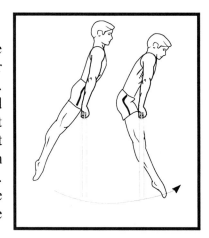

From a slightly arched front support position, the gymnast allows the legs to swing forward and under the bar and then swings back to the start position. The gymnast's legs should remain extended throughout the swing with the hips in constant contact with the bar. The grip remains stable in the support position, although the elbows may bend slightly on the forward swing of the legs. Spot the wrist and legs. Watch for bending of the arms, this may cause the gymnast to slide down off the bar if they bend the arms too much.

15. Cast Off Low Bar – Come Back to Low Bar

From a slightly arched front support position, the gymnast allows the legs to swing forward and under the bar and then swings back while pushing down with the arms on the bar causing the legs and hips to rise free from the bar to a position just below parallel to the floor. The gymnast's legs should remain extended throughout the backward swing with the seat tight and tucked under, the stomach sucked in, and the head in a neutral position relative to the body. The hips should return to the bar in a slightly arched position allowing the body to "wrap" rather than "bump" the bar in the finish position. Stand behind the bar and to the side of the gymnast. Spot the wrist and legs. Watch for excessive bending of the arms. Guide the gymnast back to the bar.

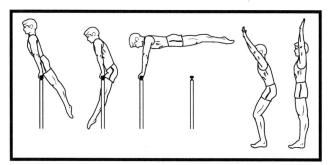

16. Cast off low bar to stand

Preparation: There must be a minimum of a 4-inch landing mat and an 8-inch landing cushion under the low bar for this skill.

From a slightly arched front support position, the gymnast allows the legs to swing forward and under the bar and then swings back while pushing down with the arms on the bar causing the legs and hips to rise free from the bar to a position just below parallel to the floor. At the peak of the cast, the gymnast pushes off the bar through his arms and chest to land on the safety landing cushion with knees slightly bent, lower back rounded, and head in neutral position with both arms extended and tight to the ears.

17. Hock swing low bar – Hands on low bar

From a stand in front of the low bar, the gymnast grasps the bar in a shoulder-width "over grip." Next, the gymnast pulls both knees up to the chest and continues to

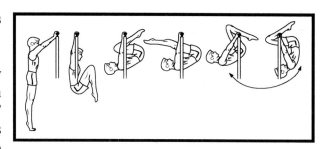

tuck up until he can extend his legs through his arms and bend his knees over the low bar. The gymnast can initiate a small swing back and forth.

Note: Spot the wrist and legs as they pass through the arms. Then place one hand on the upper back to guide the swing back and forth. Watch the gymnast's hands for grip control. Be prepared if the gymnast looses his grip or a hand slips. It is recommended to keep one hand on the gymnasts wrist at all times.

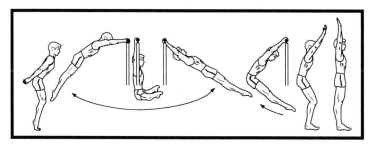

18. Glide Swing – Low Bar

From a stand in front of the low bar, the gymnast grasps the bar in a shoulder-width "over grip." Next, the gymnast pushes off the floor from a slight knee bend and lifts the legs into a seated straddle position as he swings back and forth.

19. Perch to sole hang dismount.

From the "perch position" the gymnast extends both the arms and legs as the body begins to swing backward / downward while keeping his head between his ears. As the gymnast passes under the bar and begins to swing forward / upward he quickly extends the body into a graceful arch pushing through the arms and kipping the legs forward / upward to a safety landing position.

20. Jump to sole hang dismount – straddle

Preparation: There must be a minimum of an 8-inch landing cushion under the low bar for this skill.

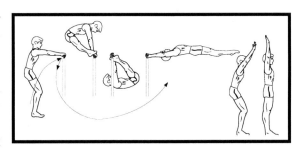

From a stand in front of the low bar on a stack of mats, the gymnast grasps the bar in a shoulder-width "over grip." Next, the gymnast jumps from the mat stack and lifts his legs into a straddled position with the balls of the feet on the bar. To finish, the gymnast swings down-forward quickly extending the legs from the bar and pushing off with his arms to finish in a standing stretch position.

Note: Initially, the instructor should spot the gymnast's wrist to make sure he does not let go of the bar early.

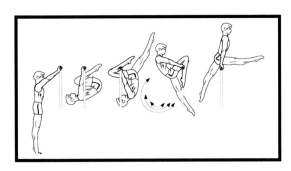

21. Single knee swing up

From a stand in front of the low bar, the gymnast grasps the bar in a shoulder-width "over grip." Next, the gymnast pulls both knees up to the chest and then extends one leg between the arms and over the bar. With the knee bent over the bar and the other leg extended the gymnast takes two to three swings and in the back uprise portion of the swing presses down on the bar with both arms to finish in a stride support. Spot the wrist and guide the bottom leg up to the stride support finish position.

22. Stride support position on low bar, [for introduction to front stride circle / mill circle)

From a stand in front of the low bar, the gymnast grasps the bar in a shoulder-width "over grip." The gymnast may do a hip pullover and cut one leg over the bar by shifting his weight to one arm while raising the other and bringing the leg on the same side over and to the front of the bar. An alternate method to finish in a stride support is to do a single knee swing up. Spot the wrist of the hand that is not cutting over the bar. The spotter may place a hand under the rear leg for support and control as the front leg cuts over the bar. Emphasize straight arms through out the skill.

23. Hip Pullover on Low Bar

From a stand in front of the low bar, the gymnast grasps the bar in a shoulder-width "over grip." Next, the gymnast pulls both legs up and over the bar, shift ting the grip backwards so the gymnast finishes in a front support on the bar. The mount may start with tucked legs or straight legs depending on the strength

of the gymnast. In addition, the gymnast may stand on a panel mat to initiate the skill. Spot from side and help the legs and lower back come over the bar while holding the wrist with one hand. Finish in straight arm support. Emphasize good form.

24. Small cast to back hip circle (tuck position)

From a stand in front of the low bar, the gymnast grasps the bar in a shoulder-width "over grip." The gymnast does a hip pullover to a support position. From a slightly arched front support position, the gymnast allows the legs to swing forward and under the bar and then swings back while pushing down with the arms on the bar causing the legs and hips to rise free from the bar to a position just below parallel to the floor. The gymnast's legs should remain extended throughout the backward swing with the seat tight and tucked under, the stomach sucked in, and the head in a neutral position relative to the body. The hips should return to the bar in a slightly arched position allowing the body to "wrap" rather than "bump" the bar in the tuck position and continue rotating around the bar to finish in a stretched position. Coach helps maintain control by holding the wrist while other hand is placed on the back to aid the gymnast around the bar. Emphasize finishing in a stretched front support.

25. Small cast to back hip circle (pike position)

Same as "small cast to back hip circle (tuck position) except the legs are piked. Coach helps maintain control by holding the wrist while other hand is placed on the back to aid the gymnast around the bar. Emphasize finishing in a stretched front support

26. Small cast to back hip circle (stretched position)

Same as "small cast to back hip circle (tuck position) except the legs are stretched. Coach helps maintain control by holding the wrist while other hand is placed on the back to aid the gymnast around the bar. Emphasize finishing in a stretched front support.

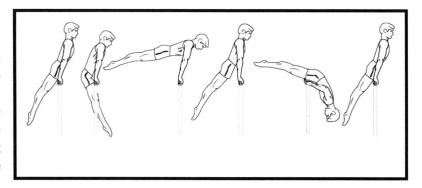

Photo courtesy of Heather Maynez

SECTION 11

Pommel Horse – Overview

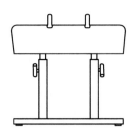

The pommel horse is one of the most difficult events for the beginner and advanced beginner student. It is an event that has limited success and must be broken down into parts which include basic static skills also known as held skills. The reason is strength because pommel horse requires strength to support oneself using the upper body extremities which include the arms, shoulders and wrists. Young male gymnasts take longer to develop strength in these areas compared to young female athletes. During a pommel horse routine the gymnasts has to support his entire body weight by his hands throughout the entire routine. His upper body must be conditioned and strong enough to complete his exercise. A strong middle core is also required in order to maintain body tightness. You as the instructor must focus on basics with the least number of body segments necessary to perform the skill, appropriate body line and muscular tension to maintain form necessary for the skill with adequate range of motion or flexibility. Strength is a key component and should be included during training and after training in the conditioning program.

Swing

During a pommel horse routine most skills require a constant fluid swinging motion. When watching a high level gymnast or an Olympic level routine one can easily see that swing moves are large and flowing through out the entire routine. In the learning phases, coaches should introduce very basic static positions first. These positions will help build strength in the upper and mid sections of the body. Once the class has shown some level of proficiency they can gradually move into the single-leg pendulum swing skills.

Basic Positions

Front Support   Rear Support   Stride Support

Pommel Horse Introduction

In the introduction phase the 3 basic positions listed above should be practiced on the floor and mushroom first. Lead up skills for pommel horse will have positive carry over into other boys events. Many of the skills are similar and have the same name. First introduce a front, rear and stride support. Emphasize form and good body positions with head in neutral position and body tight throughout.

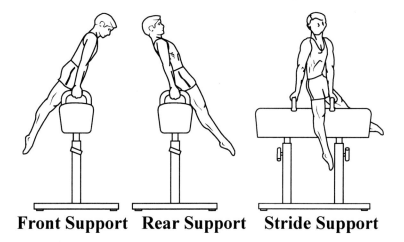

Front Support   Rear Support   Stride Support

Mushroom

The mushroom is a training device that may be placed on a mat or positioned on a low base of support. It is an excellent training tool and aids in all levels of instruction. You will see high level skills and sequences trained on the mushroom before they are transferred onto a pommel horse. Also used at the entry level competitions for boys!

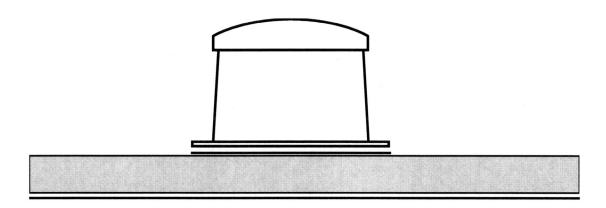

Pommel Horse – Level 1

Pommel Horse Floor Drills

1. Front Straight Body Support –
(On the Floor)
Start by having the gymnast kneel on the floor exercise mat with both hands in front of his chest, have him lift the hips up and fully extend the body into a straight position. Emphasize shoulders directly over hands and straight arms with pointed toes. Spot the arms and extended leg for support and balance.

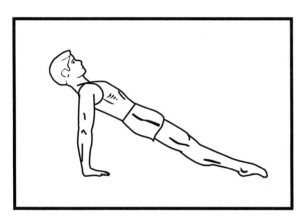

2. Rear Support –
(On the Floor)
Have the gymnast start in a sit on the floor exercise mat with hands behind his seat while extending the legs and raising his hips encourage good body tightness and straight legs. Remind him to point his feet all the way through his toes. To maintain balance the gymnast must squeeze the hips and torso tight. Spot from the side.

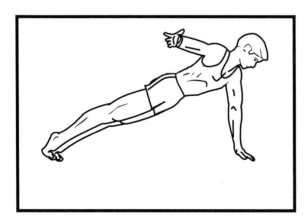

3. Support on One Arm
(On the Floor)
Have the gymnast start in front support position with both hands in front of chest, lift the right hand out to right side while remaining in a straight body position. Emphasize shoulders over the base hand for support with body tight. Head remains neutral. Spot from the side and emphasize tight hips and torso. Rotate to other arm.

Mushroom Skills

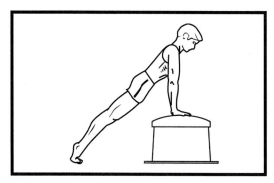

4. Front Straight Body Support –
Start by having the gymnast with both hands in front of his chest on top of the mushroom, have him lift the hips up and fully extend the body into a straight position. Emphasize shoulders directly over hands and straight arms with pointed toes. Spot the arms and extended leg for support and balance.

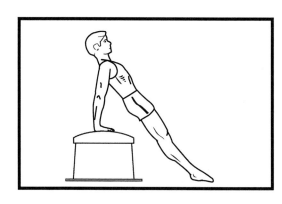

5. Rear Support –
Have the gymnast start in a sit on the floor exercise mat with hands behind his seat while extending the legs and raising his hips encourage good body tightness and straight legs. Remind him to point his feet all the way through his toes. To maintain balance the gymnast must squeeze the hips and torso tight. Spot from the side.

6. Support on Left Arm
Have the gymnast start in front support position with both hands in front of chest, lift the right hand out to right side while remaining in a straight body position. Emphasize shoulders over the base hand for support with body tight. Head remains neutral. Spot from the side and emphasize tight hips and torso.

7. Support on Right Arm
Have the gymnast start in front support position with both hands in front of chest, lift the left hand out to left side while remaining in a straight body position. Emphasize shoulders over the base hand for support with body tight. Head remains neutral. Spot from the side and emphasize tight hips and torso.

8. Walk Around the Mushroom

Have the gymnast start in front support position with both hands in front of chest, lift the right hand (or the right hand) out to side while remaining in a straight body position and walk around the side of the low mushroom. Alternate hands by lifting them up one at a time as the gymnast travels around and be sure to stay on top of the mushroom. This is an excellent drill for practicing hand changes. Emphasize shoulders over the base hand for support with body tight. Head remains neutral. Spot from the side if needed and emphasize tight hips and torso. Rotate all the way around until back to starting position. Practice this drill over and over. Always check for proper matting under the mushroom.

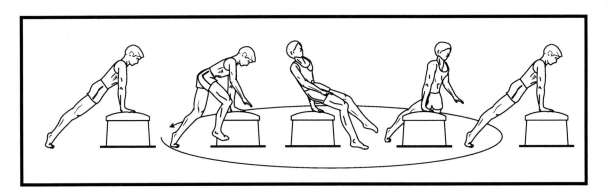

9. Hop Around the Mushroom with 360 Rotation

Hop from front support position to rear support position around the mushroom (180 degree hop). Finish 360 rotation by walking around the mushroom back to the original starting position.

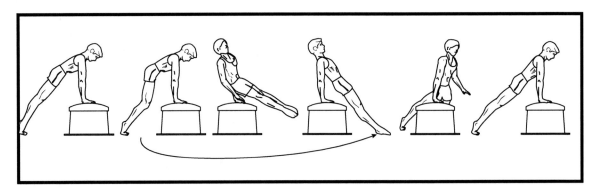

10. Three Quarter Hop (270 degree hop)

Three quarter hop of 270 degrees around the mushroom. Finish 360 rotation by walking around mushroom back to starting position. For learning purposes, sliding on the bottom and legs is acceptable to assist in learning how to finish the complete circle.

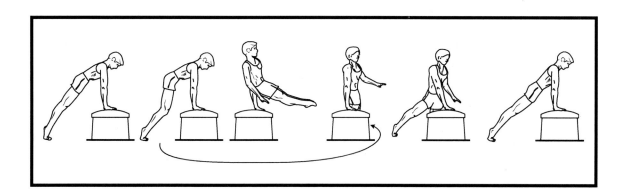

Pommel Horse Basics

11. Front Support   **12. Rear Support**

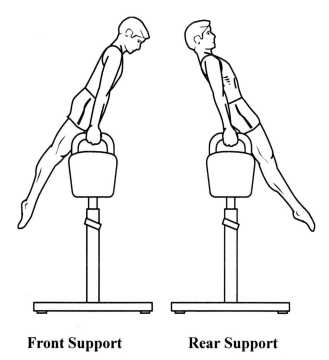

Front Support   Rear Support

11. Front Support   **12: Rear Support:**

The fundamental techniques for the front and rear support positions are as follows:

1.   A straight body line is the desired position for both the front an rear body positions. The front support should have the shoulders slightly forward and the rear support have the shoulders slightly backward. A good way to explain this to the gymnast is to use the numbers on a clock with 1:00 position for front support and 11:00 for rear support.

2.   The head position should remain neutral or in a natural position for both supports.

3.   Grasp the pommels at center or slightly forward while in front support position and at center or slightly backward in rear support.

4.   Tighten the arms slightly inward to station the shoulders.

5.   The tighter the static body positions the better for muscle memory.

13.   Front Straddle Support Swings – (With or without lifting hand off the pommels.)

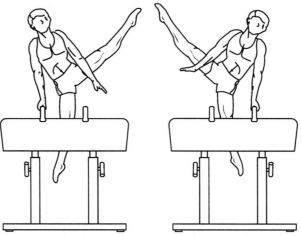

14. Rear Straddle Support Swings - (With or without lifting hands off pommels.)

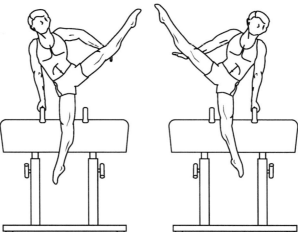

Photo Courtesy of Heather Maynez

USA Coaches Certification, Inc.

SECTION 12

Still Rings - Overview

The still rings as this event is commonly known today can be a fun and exciting event for both boys and girls. Mixed classes can rotate to the low rings and feel somewhat successful the first day. Often observed on play ground swing sets are children playing and swinging on the outdoor rings. Although the most common observed activity on the play ground rings was a child running back and forth under the rings swinging as high as they could. Swinging back and forth has the potential to cause serious injury to the gymnast if they should loose their grip and fall. Gymcert therefore recommends NO running under the rings and NO swinging back and forth in a gymnastics class. A typical gymnastics school has ring stations with "skill cushion" mats directly under the rings. Some even have additional mats under the rings for added safety. It is imperative that there is proper matting under the rings and that the rings are head height or shoulder height of the students. It is common to see the floor matting area raised with several mats to bring the rings closer to the students and as close to shoulder height as possible. This is especially seen if the rings are fixed at a set height and can not be lowered with their straps. The still rings are meant to remain as still as possible with no or little movement or swing. The mat set up mentioned above is safe for skills that are static and non-moving.

Two Types of Motion
Static and Dynamic motion are the two types of motion seen on the rings. Training skills for the beginner level gymnast should focus on "static" moves first. Static skills are those positions that are considered as strength moves and are held in a stationary, still position. Dynamic skills are those that have motion. When introducing static holds to young students be sure to place your spotting hand around their wrist/wrists just in case they loose grip.

Swinging Skills
The nature of a pendulum swing takes the gymnast back and forth across the mat but if the student losses his grip the angle of the swing, speed and dynamics of the swing could send him flying potentially off the end of the mats. Experienced ring coaches are very familiar with the words "peeling off". Pealing off the equipment means that the gymnast looses his grip and can not hold on thus having a non controlled release. Pealing of the rings has the potential to cause a serious injury to the gymnast. Gymcert would like to caution the reader as the professional to be extremely "safety minded" when instructing at this event and to stay "proactive" and constantly aware of the students hands at all times while taking his turn on the rings. It is recommended that spotting or holding onto the gymnast's wrist or using "hands on" spotting is always the preferred practice for spotting. Swinging skills used in the rings requires adequate upper body strength and should be taught under close care and supervision of an experienced instructor. Correct technique should be emphasized along with proper strength training. Improper training can place undue stress in young gymnast's joints and thus cause injury. Caution should be used when introducing "swing" type movements.

Hands on Spotting

GYMCERT Advisory Board recommends "hands on" spotting. When you are learning or practicing your spotting techniques you should work along side or shadow an experienced instructor or team level coach. Double spotting a skill with another instructor is a safe way to practice your spotting skills. Continue to do this until you are confident and proficient in all the skills that you are teaching. It is also good practice to spot skills on gymnasts or students that can already successfully complete the skill. This will allow the instructor the opportunity to use a different or updated spotting technique for "spotting" that particular move. Never wing a spot! If you are not 100% confident in your spotting skill – DO NOT attempt to spot the skill. It is all right to ask a more experienced coach for help and guidance when you are not experienced in a particular spot!

Core Conditioning

It is imperative that some sort of core conditioning be included in your training program. As quoted by Robert Dvorak, in the 1985 USGF Gymnastics Safety Manual, "Coaches should be cautioned that body looseness is an essential critical error on rings, and could cause lower back problems particularly when performing the more advanced skills. Skills require a large amount of swing should be treated with due respect because of the tremendous forces being generated. Performers should be made aware that the greatest danger of slipping off the rings occurs as the body passes through the vertical hanging position. Should this occur, the body would be rotating rapidly through a very low trajectory and the potential for serious injury becomes high. Such a predicament is almost impossible to spot. Consequently, the best prevention can be found in adequately mastering the technique of swinging. Ample matting, appropriately placed, is also vitally important."

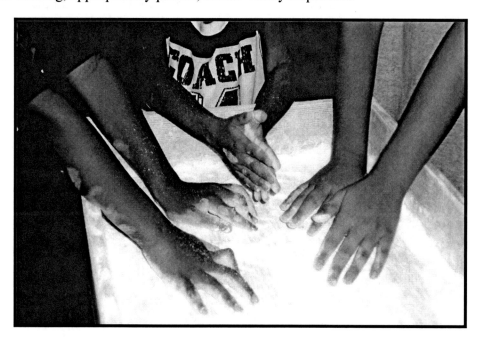

Still Rings Level 1

Every gymnast should be introduced to the basic body positions for the still rings. Practice basic positions and review often. The coach should always stay by the gymnast's side and use "hands on" spotting. Always check the height of the rings and the matting under the apparatus before beginning the class. It is your responsibility to check to make sure your teaching area is ready for class before you begin.

1. Straight Body Hang

From a static hang on the rings, the gymnast hangs with feet together, legs straight and the toes together and pointed. The gymnast controls his hang by squeezing stomach and seat tight. Spot by standing close to the rings with a hand on the gymnast's wrist. Remind the gymnast to stay tight and to try not to swing.

2. Hang in Tuck Position

This skill is the same as a "straight body hang," except the legs are bent at the knees and hips. This skill can be practiced at the same time as the straight body hang just by asking the student to change his lower body position. Spot the wrist and the legs with one had and the lower back or thigh with the other hand. This will help keep the swing down to a minimum. Stand next to rings at all times.

3. Hang in L Hold

Start by having the gymnast hang in a straight body position. Then slowly raise straight legs to a 90 degree position in front of body. Spot by supporting the gymnast's legs under the thigh while encouraging the student to hold their legs out in a tight straight position with as little swing as possible. Coach should be in a ready position spotting the students wrist and legs.

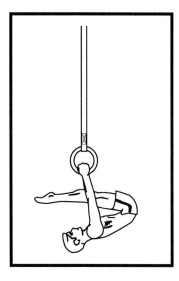

4. Inverted Pike Hold

Start by having the gymnast hang in a straight body hang. Then slowly raise straight legs to a 90 degree position in front of the body. See #3 illustrations then slowly direct the gymnast to rotate backward while maintaining a tight, controlled pike position. Have the gymnast try to compress his body as tight as possible. Nose as close to the knees as possible while keeping form. The point of rotation is around the hands. Emphasize control and good form throughout the entire movement. Legs together and toes pointed. Spot the back and shoulder area and be sure to guide and direct the rotation direction with your free spotting arm.

5. Inverted Hang

Have the gymnast start in a tucked V-sit with arms up next to the ears   and slowly unroll backwards while extending the legs. To maintain balance the gymnast must squeeze the hips and torso tight. Spot from the side of the gymnast. Spot by placing hand under shoulder and use free hand to help guide the legs to the inverted hanging position.

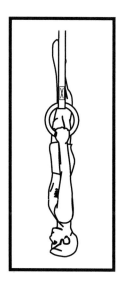

6. Skin-the-cat Hang

Start by having the gymnast hang in a straight body hang. Then slowly raise tucked or straight legs to a 90 degree position in front of the body. See #3 illustrations then slowly direct the gymnast to rotate backward while maintaining a tight, controlled pike position. Have the gymnast continue through the inverted pike position and then extend through an open shoulder position with the feet extended or pointed toward the floor. The point of rotation is around the hands and shoulders. Emphasize control and good form throughout the entire movement. Legs together and toes pointed. The gymnast opens his hips and shoulder angles as much as he safely can without over straining his shoulders. A long hollow body with as straight line as possible. Spot the back and shoulder area and be sure to guide the legs with your free spotting hand while also supporting them.

RING SWINGS

7. Forward Swing

The key to the forward swing is a tight body in good alignment. On the front swing, the legs should be "scooped" forward to a hollowed position. Rings are spread wide and turned outward. Focus by looking toward the rings. Spot from the side in a ready position. Spotting the swing by placing hands on the stomach and thighs or lower back is recommended. This skill must be carefully spotted and taught under the direct supervision of a competent spotter.

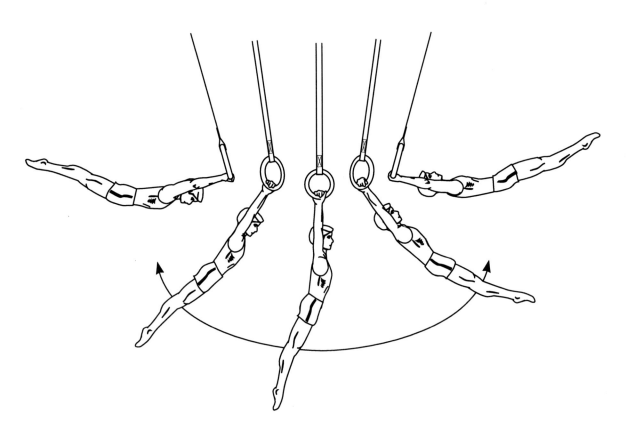

8. Backward Swing.

The backward swing is taught at the same time as the forward swing. The body should remain tight through out the entire movement. On the backward swing, the rings should be kept diagonally to the sides. The head should be looking with eyes focused on the rings. Practice basic swing with attention to body position and details. This skill is the building block toward success on the rings. Spot the legs and back for control through out the swing.

9. Swing to Inverted Hang

Straight body front and back swings as in #7 and #8 except on the front swing as gymnast hollows it is necessary to break shoulder angle by pulling hands to hips until the body in a straight body inverted hang. Spot from the side of the gymnast and watch the hand position closely and spot the body as it rises and be prepared to control the swing.

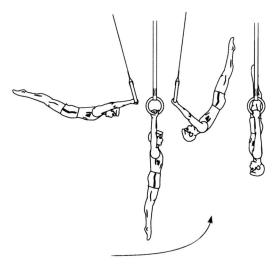

10. Swing to Inverted Hang, to Pike Hang, to Skin the Cat Dismount

Once the gymnast has become familiar with the skills in the Level 1 ring section challenge them to put a few of the skills together in combination. Combine them into a sequence or a short routine. Gymcert recommends that the coach emphasis a good start position and a held finish position at both the beginning and end of the sequence. Remind the gymnast of the previously mentioned technical points especially to pike tighter in the inverted L hang position and extend more in the shoulders and hips during the skin-the- cat portion. Spot from the side and be in a ready position at all times. Keep a close eye on the hands of the gymnast. Spot from the side and help guide through the positions and on the landing.

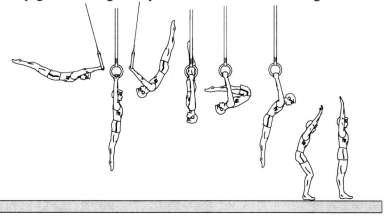

Conditioning & Flexibility

12. Inlocate and Dislocate

Inlocate and Dislocate: From a standing position have the gymnast take hold of a wooden dowel or PVC pipe with both hands in an over grip position. Hands should be placed as close as comfortably suitable for each gymnast and will vary due to individual's flexibility. Instruct the gymnast to rotate his arms back and forth over head while keeping arms straight. If the gymnast needs to bend his arms then the grip is too close and should be widened. Shoulder flexibility is important on the bars and should not be over looked. Having several wooden dowels is common in a training setting and aids when incorporating group flexibility training. Do not lean forward; keep body upright with shoulders pressed down and back. Spot from a ready position and guide the training bar slowly back and forth. This movement should be slow and deliberate.

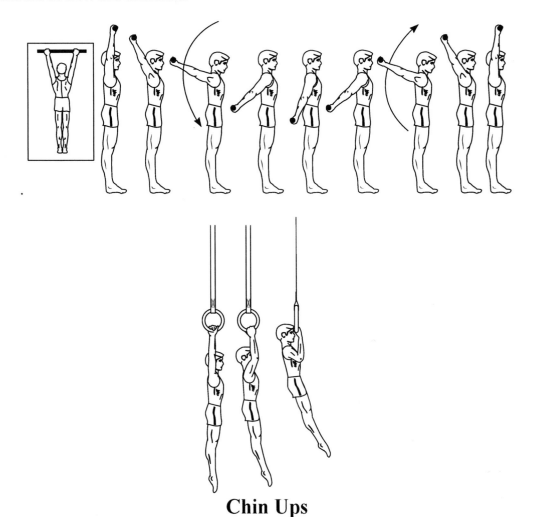

Chin Ups

Spot the gymnast from the side as he executes his chin ups. Start out one or two and build the numbers slowly. Keep the rings as still as possible.

SECTION 13

Parallel Bars - Overview

The parallel bars also know as "P" Bars is similar to the other boy's events in that it requires both technique and upper body strength. A typical gymnastics school may have a low parallette station with "skill cushion" mats directly under it or a competition parallel bar set-up with mats built up underneath as well as on the ends. Some stations will place additional mats under the parallel bars for added safety. It is imperative that there is proper matting under the parallel bars and that they are set at an appropriate height for the level of the class. It is common to see the floor matting area raised with several mats to bring the "P" bars closer to the students and as close to chest height as possible. Parallel bar routines are made up skills that swing about the hands and shoulders of the athlete. Moves are seen both above and below the parallel bars. There are a variety of moves that make up a routine. There will be a variety of twisting moves as well as turning skills with salto and flight skills with release and regrasps. Exciting to say the least!!

Strength and Readiness
Instructors of Level 1 students should first focus on the basic "held" or static positions. These moves are non-swinging skills which aid in the students strength development. Strength is needed in both the upper body and mid section of the body along with balance and form. All basic body positions should be mastered before moving on to any swinging type skills. Olympic coach, Fred Roethlisberger, suggests that "A performer should not be permitted to swing higher or more vigorously that that which his strength and skill can safely control. Coaches should be cautioned that poor mechanics and improper training are especially critical errors on the parallel bars. Performers should be aware that the greatest danger on slipping off the parallel bars occurs just as the body passes through the vertical swinging position." Spotting the parallel bars is done either from above or below the bars and depends on the skill being performed. Always think "safety" first and always when establishing your lesson plans for your classes. Remember that correct use of skill progressions is critical to a safe learning environment.

Swinging Skills
The nature of a pendulum swing takes the gymnast back and forth across the parallel bars but if the student losses his grip the angle of the swing, speed and dynamics of the swing could send him flying potentially off the end of the mats. Be aware that a gymnast "pealing off" the P-bars could end with a potential injury. Common injuries include wrist, arm and elbow fractures and dislocations. Pealing off the equipment means that the gymnast looses his grip and can not hold on thus having a non controlled release. Gymcert would like to caution the reader as the professional to be extremely "safety minded" when instructing at this event and to stay "proactive" and constantly aware of the students hands at all times while taking his turn on the parallel bars. Gymcert recommends that spotting or holding onto the gymnast's wrist

or using "hands on" spotting is always the preferred practice for spotting. Swinging skills used in the rings requires adequate upper body strength and should be taught under close care and supervision of an experienced instructor. Correct technique should be emphasized along with proper strength training. Improper training can place undue stress in young gymnast's joints and thus cause injury. Caution should be used when introducing all "swing" type movements.

Hands on Spotting

Gymcert recommends "hands on" spotting. When you are learning or practicing your spotting techniques you should work along side or shadow an experienced instructor or team level coach. Double spotting a skill with another instructor is a safe way to practice your spotting skills. Continue to do this until you are confident and proficient in all the skills that you are teaching. It is also good practice to spot skills on gymnasts or students that can already successfully complete the skill. This will allow the instructor the opportunity to use a different or updated spotting technique for "spotting" that particular move. Never wing a spot! If you are not 100% confident in your spotting skill – DO NOT attempt to spot the skill. It is alright to ask a more experienced coach for help and guidance when you are not experienced in a particular spot!

Spotting on the parallel bars will become complicated as the student progresses. They may have moves that pass above and below the bars which will call for an experienced coach to spot. The spotter's hands have to reach from below and through the parallel bars and there is danger that the student could land on the spotters arms. The instructor should be able to spot comfortably and confidently. As skills become more advanced an overhead belt or spotting platform may be needed. Double spotting a skill is always a sure safe method so don't hesitate to do so!

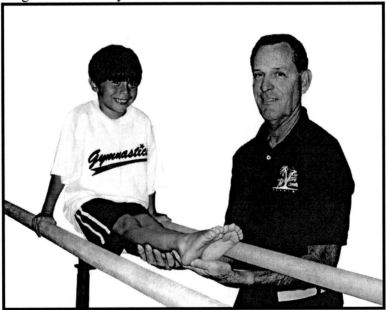

Coach Bob Ward
(Photo courtesy of Rita Brown)

Parallel Bars Level 1

Every gymnast should be introduced to the basic body positions for the parallel bars. Practice basic positions and review them often. The coach should always stay by the gymnast's side and use "hands on" spotting. Always check the height of the parallel bars and the matting under the apparatus before beginning the class. It is your responsibility to check to make sure your teaching area is ready for class before you begin.

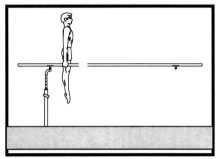

1. Straight Arm Support
(Body straight in vertical position)

From a static shoulder hang on the parallel bars, the gymnast hangs with feet together, legs straight and the toes together and pointed. The gymnast controls his hang by squeezing stomach, seat and legs tight. Spot by standing close to the bars with a hand on the gymnast's wrist and/or legs depending on the strength of the student. Remind the gymnast to stay tight and to try not to swing.

2. Straight Arm Support in Tuck Position
This skill is the same as a "straight body shoulder hang," except the legs are bent at the knees and hips. This skill can be practiced at the same time as the straight body hang just by asking the student to change his lower body position. Spot the wrist and the legs with one had and the lower back or thigh with the other hand. This will help keep the swing down to a minimum. Stand next to bars at all times.

3. Straight Arm Support Hold Position
Start by having the gymnast hang in a straight body shoulder hang position. Then instruct the gymnast to slowly raise his straight legs to a 90 degree position in front of body. Spot by supporting the gymnast's legs under the thigh while encouraging the student to hold their legs out in a tight straight position with as little swing as possible. Coach should be in a ready position spotting the students wrist and legs.

4. Front Straight Body Support –
(On the Floor)
Start by having the gymnast kneel on the floor exercise mat with both hands in front of his chest, have him lift the hips up and fully extend the body into a straight position. Emphasize shoulders directly over hands and straight arms with pointed toes. Spot the arms and extended leg for support and balance.

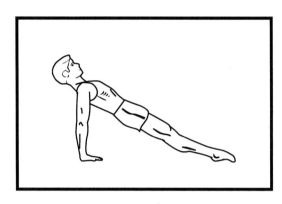

5. Rear Support –
(On the Floor)
Have the gymnast start in a sit on the floor exercise mat with hands behind his seat while extending the legs and raising his hips encourage good body tightness and straight legs. Remind him to point his feet all the way through his toes. To maintain balance the gymnast must squeeze the hips and torso tight. Spot from the side.

Swing Movements on Parallel Bars

6. Straight Arm Support Swings

The gymnast begins support swings from a support position. Have the gymnast start with a controlled kicking of the legs forward and upward creating a scoop shape on the upswing. On the back swing the body falls passively until it passes through vertical. After passing through the vertical position the legs begin a controlled kicking action backward and upward until the chest begins to pull in slightly. (The greater the distance between the arms and the trunk the greater the swing). It is important that the instructor remind the gymnast to master the swing technique with small swings and gradually build to large swings. Spot from the side of the bars and on top of spotting plat form or mats if necessary.

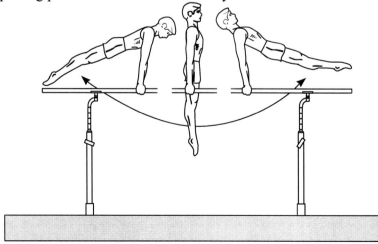

7. Straight Arm Support Swings into Straddle
The key to the forward swing is a tight body in good alignment. On the front swing, the legs should be "scooped" forward to a hollowed position. Focus by looking straight at the end of the P-bars. Spot from the side in a ready position. Spotting the swing by placing hands on the stomach and thighs or lower back is recommended. This skill must be carefully spotted and taught under the direct supervision of a competent spotter.

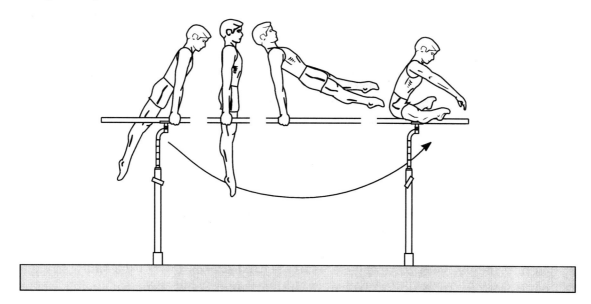

Straight Arm Support Swings into Straddle (traveling down the bars)

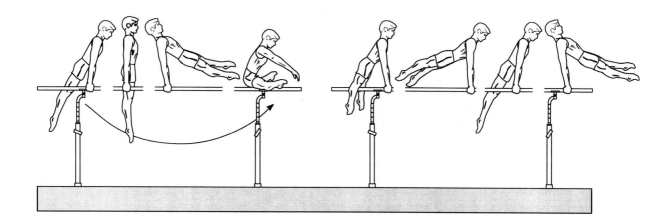

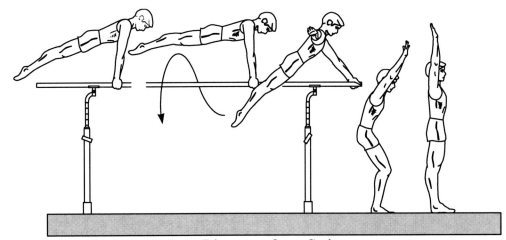

Rear Dismount from Swing

8. Rear Dismount from Swing

The backward swing is taught at the same time as the forward swing. The body should remain tight through out the entire movement. On the front swing, the legs should be "scooped" forward to a hollowed position. Focus by looking straight at the end of the P-bars. Spot from the side that the dismount is on. Spot the back swing by placing hands on the stomach, thighs or knee area. Have the gymnast regrasp the bar with the left hand as his body descends toward the finish landing position on the right side of the bars. The right arm is shoulder height straight out to the side. This skill must be carefully spotted and taught under the direct supervision of a competent spotter.

Spot the legs and back for control through out the swing.

Photo Courtesy of Heather Maynez

SECTION 14

Trampoline - Overview

If any gymnastics device could be described as magnetic, the trampoline would have to be it. Upon entering the facility, young gymnasts make a beeline for it right away. The trampoline is fun. The gymnast can practice several skills with less wear and tear on the body. It is a great device for practicing aerial or spatial awareness of new skills. The trampoline is also where the majority of safety rules is ignored and as a result could lead to potentially catastrophic injury for the gymnast.

No matter its shape, size, or name, a trampoline, mini-tramp, tumble-tramp, or double-mini tramp is a device that requires specific supervision and the undivided attention of the instructor.

Often due to other programs in the facility, like birthday parties, mixed messages are sent to young gymnasts. During the party, normal safety rules are suspended (in some programs) and activities take place on the tramp that would never occur in class. Use of the tramp for fun during parties can be achieved by outlining safety procedures like the stop bounce technique, the no somersault rule, and only one gymnast at a time. It is also important that all gymnasts in class or parties understand they should never attempt a new or difficult skill without permission and qualified supervision.

Review safe landing procedures for the pit with all gymnasts, if your tumble tramp or trampoline allows dismounting into a foam or resi-pit. Safety first and always!

Instructors, keep a close eye on head alignment (neutral position), especially in younger gymnasts. It is quite easy for a gymnast who is relaxed to create a whiplash effect with the head and neck if they do not focus on keeping the head in a neutral position. In addition, it is not a good idea for the Level 1 gymnast to do any form of knee drop as a slight arch in the back on landing could cause serious pain and make the gymnast feel as if the wind has been knocked out of his.

The Level 1 Certification program for trampoline is designed to teach trampoline skills in a safe and progressive manner so your class members have a fun and rewarding experience.

The Level 1 Certification program for Trampoline begins on the next page.

Trampoline – Level 1

Trampoline is a *specific supervision* activity.   No person should use this device without qualified supervision.   The following are safety guidelines for trampoline:

- One person at a time.
- Performer must stay in the MIDDLE of the tramp at all times.
- To finish a turn, always STOP / CHECK BOUNCE, then walk to the side and carefully return to the floor.
- No front or back somersaults, or front or back drops at Level 1 or Level 2.
- Instructor must be ready to spot at all times. No sitting or relaxing on the edge of the tramp. Crossing your arms in front of your body displays a negative image.

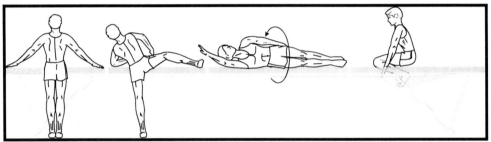

1. Climb on and off tramp (correctly and safely).

 (With no side platform or stairs :) To mount the tramp, the gymnast should hold the side and lift one leg up and over, after which the gymnast can roll sideways and then proceed to stand in the middle of the tramp.

To dismount, the gymnast should perform a stop bounce and then walk to the side, reach down with one hand for control to hold the tramp, and then sit with the legs over the edge of the tramp and turn sideways to let the legs drop to the floor while maintaining balance with one hand still on the edge of the tramp.

**2. 10 Bounces with control
in the middle – stop with control – arm emphasis**

The gymnast starts in the center of the tramp with both arms at the side, and then bends his knees and jumps up while extending his arms upward. Returning to the tramp the gymnast should circle his arms backward and down and land on the tramp with tight legs, stomach sucked in, and lower back tight to achieve another controlled bounce with arms extended  upward. Repeat the sequence from the "tight leg" landing for repeated bounces or bend the legs to stop the bounce. Spread spotters out around tramp and spot from a ready position.

Complete 10 bounces and then demonstrate a controlled stop by bending the knees.

3. Bounce and stop with control (Stop Bounce or Check Bounce)

Using the bounce technique already described, the instructor should teach the gymnast to stop on command by simply bending the knees upon landing from a bounce. Speaking clearly, "One, two, three, stop!" will prepare the gymnast to bend his knees on the appropriate bounce and absorb the power from the tramp.

4. Tuck jump

At the peak of each bounce, in the center of the tramp, using proper bounce technique, the gymnast should quickly tuck his knees to his chest, and then extend his feet again to land and bounce or stop bounce. Spread spotters out around tramp and spot from a ready position.

5. Straddle jump (legs slightly piked forward)

At the peak of each bounce, in the center of the tramp, using proper bounce technique, the gymnast should quickly lift the legs into a straddle position with knees tight and toes pointed. The legs should be slightly piked forward in the straddle jump. The gymnast should finish by extending his feet again to land and bounce or stop bounce.

Spotting Tips: Spread spotters out around tramp and spot from a ready position.

6. Tuck jump, straddle jump – stop bounce.

At the peak of the first bounce, in the center of the tramp, the gymnast should quickly tuck his knees to his chest, and then extend his feet again to land. On the second bounce, the gymnast should quickly lift the legs into a straddle position with  knees tight and toes pointed and then extend his feet again to land and stop bounce by bending his knees. Spread spotters out around tramp and spot from a ready position.

7. Star jump

At the peak of the bounce, in the center of the tramp, using proper bounce technique, the gymnast should quickly lift the arms into the 10:00 and 2:00 positions while at the same time lifting the legs into the 4:00 and 8:00 positions. Use stop bounce technique to control the landing. Spread spotters out around tramp and spot from a ready position.

8. Pike jump

At the peak of the bounce, in the center of the tramp, using proper bounce technique, the gymnast should quickly lift the legs into a pike position with knees tight and toes pointed. The chest should remain upright and the gymnast may touch his knees with both hands. Use the stop bounce technique to finish the skill. Spread spotters out around tramp and spot from a ready position.

9. Jump ½ turn
Jump 1/1 turn

Body tightness is the key to any bounce with a turn. Leaning the body in any direction during the turn will cause the gymnast to bounce crooked and possibly fall off the tramp. At the peak of a stretched body position bounce, the gymnast has simply to look quickly to the left or right for a spot behind his to complete a half turn. A full turn can be learned by incrementally adding rotation to the half turn (I.E. ½ turn plus 10 degrees of turn, then 20 degrees, until a full turn is completed.). Start with smaller bounces until the turn technique is perfected. Use stop bounce technique to control the landing. Spread spotters out around tramp and spot from a ready position.

10. Seat drop to stand

From a standing position, have the gymnast initiate a small bounce. At the peak of the bounce, the gymnast will lift both feet similar to the pike jump and hold them in this position allowing his to land

on his seat and back of legs simultaneously. The hands should be on the tramp beside the gymnast's thighs with fingers pointed toward the toes. It is important that the gymnast's stomach be sucked in and lower back slightly rounded but tight to prevent jamming the lower back. On the resulting bounce, the gymnast should push off the tramp with both hands and reach up to land in stretch position.

11. Seat drop ½ turn to stand.

Follow the directions from "seat drop to stand" and upon the return bounce from the seat drop as the arms are reaching to stretch position simply have the gymnast look right or left (depending on twist preference) directly in back of them to complete the half turn to stand.

Spot: Spread spotters out around tramp and spot from a ready position.

12. Tuck jump extend to seat drop – extend to straddle and return to stand.

From a stretched jump, then a bounce, have the gymnast quickly tuck the knees to the chest, and then extend the legs into a pike position; land in a seat drop on the tramp. On the following bounce reach up with the arms, lift the legs into a straddle jump position, and then extend the legs to land in a stop bounce. Spread spotters out around tramp and spot from a ready position.

Trampoline Insurance: Trampolines may require special insurance coverage and may not be included under your policy. Gymnastics professionals and club managers/owners should investigate whether their current insurance policy covers trampoline and or tumble track use.

Maintenance: Trampolines should be inspected prior to each use. Defective or worn parts should be identified and replaced. Look for holes, tears, or separated webs on the trampoline bed. Deterioration of the stitching or sagging bed should be reported and fixed.

Mini Trampolines: Should be introduced with extreme care. They are not a typical piece of equipment and are not recommended for level 1 class. Spotting a gymnast who is performing on a small mini is very difficult due to the relatively powerful bounces resulting from the running approach.

Extra Safety: Landing or additional matting at the end of the trampoline should be at least as high as the bed.

SECTION 15

Conditioning – Level 1

Conditioning

While there are several components to conditioning, and appropriate conditioning varies with the sport, the focus for Conditioning Level 1 is on strength and flexibility. Strength is needed to enable the gymnast to propel, support, and rotate himself through a variety of skills with control. Flexibility is also important so the gymnast can demonstrate a dynamic range of motion in his skills without injuring the muscles. Broadly speaking, the gymnast should be as strong as possible through as broad a range of motion on each joint as possible. The instructor is encouraged to incorporate the strength skills listed here within the weekly lesson plan and the flexibility exercises illustrated in the Floor Exercise section.

Level 1 Flexibility Skills (see Floor Exercise)
(to be performed after a cardio-warm up)

- Roll out ankles, wrists, neck, and shoulders
- Splits (right & left) 120-140 degrees (30 – 60 seconds each)
- Seated Straddle (Closed position stretching for 30 –60 seconds each to the right leg, left leg, and finally chest to the ground in the center.)
- Seated Pike (Closed position stretching bring the chest to the knees with a flat back and tight knees.)
- Straddle Split 120 degrees (facing the wall, straddle the legs and scoot the hips forward until the legs are out to the sides and the chest and stomach are flat against the wall.
- Bridge (see description under Floor Exercise)
- Shoulder Stand (see description under Floor Exercise)

Level 1 Strength

1. 20 sit-ups (build up to 20)
From layout (supine) position, bend the knees until the feet are flat on the floor. Sit up by pulling through the abdominal muscles until the chest touches the knees, and then repeat until repetitions are complete. Arms may be extended or bent at the elbows so fingers lightly touch the ears. Spot upper back when helping a gymnast to complete a sit-up.

2. 6 push-ups

From a prone position, bend the arms and place the hands flat on the ground next to the shoulders. Maintain a straight body line and extend the arms to push up to straight, but not locked arms, and then slowly lower to start position. Repeat until repetitions are complete. Emphasize good body position. If push ups are too difficult the gymnast may bend at the knees and execute a bent knee push up. Increase number of push ups by the level of each class or group of student. Emphasize straight body line from knee to shoulder with hands directly under the shoulders.

3. 6 arch-ups

From prone position, keeping the head between the arms, lift the arms, head, and chest from the floor while simultaneously lifting the heels, calves, and thighs until only the stomach remains in contact with the floor. Maintain a graceful arch briefly then lower to the floor. Repeat until repetitions are complete.

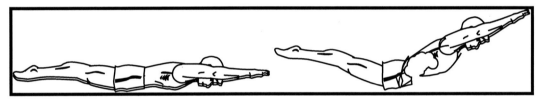

4. Pike stretch – fingertips touching toes or floor if standing – 15 sec.

From stretch position, slowly bend at the waist, keeping legs straight, until the fingertips touch the toes or floor if gymnast is in a stand position.. Hold this position for 15 seconds. Repeat.

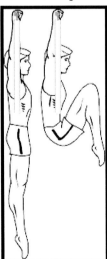

5. Tuck L – 2 seconds

From a long hang position on bars, slowly roll the seat under as the knees are tucked to the chest and the heels are brought to the back of the thighs. Hold for two seconds. Repeat.

6. Punch jumps – 45 seconds

On the floor exercise mat, starting from the position of attention, the gymnast bends their legs and jumps as high as possible with a strong arm lift. The landing requires tight legs so the gymnast may punch through the floor and get a good rebound to land with bent legs once again. Repeat until repetitions are complete.

7. 5 squat jumps

Starting from a squat position with the arms raised next to the ears, the gymnast explodes into a stretch jump, then carefully lands, and lowers into the squat position. Continue until repetitions are complete.

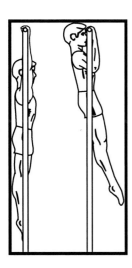

8. 1 pull up

From a long hang position on the bars with palms facing away from the body and arms shoulder width apart, pull up with arms (keeping the body straight) until the chin rises above the level of the bar. Lower slowly back to start position. Spot from behind lifting at the waist.

9. L hang or leg lift – bars

From a long hang position on the bars with palms facing away from the body and arms shoulder width apart, pull the toes to the high bar while keeping the legs straight by using the lower abdominal and hip flexor muscles. Hold in L position for 10 seconds/ Lower slowly back to start position. Spot the wrist and the legs as the lift upward.

10. Leg lifts – floor – below horizontal – 15 seconds (forward, backward, sideward)

Starting with arms in high crown position, lift one leg forward until almost parallel with the floor (keeping the leg straight), then lower to the floor and repeat by lifting the leg backward in a similar fashion, and finally to the side; holding at the peak of motion for a brief second before returning the leg to the ground. Repeat the leg lift sequence of forward, backward, sideways on each leg for fifteen seconds.

11. Run – 1 minute

In a clear area of the floor exercise or up and down the vault runway, run using proper arm and leg synchronization to get the blood flowing to all the muscle tissues of the body.

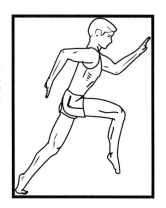

12. 5 inlocate-dislocates (with stick)

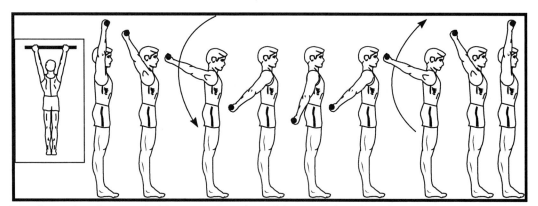

Stand on the floor. Hold a wooden dowel in your hands with your arms about 12 inches from the sides of your body. Slowly raise the dowel above and then behind your head until your shoulders are able to swivel comfortably (dislocate) and the dowel is now behind your body and you can lower your arms backward. Reverse the process to inlocate your arms. Note: Start with your arms wide on the dowel and gradually work them closer over time to better stretch your shoulders without injury.

SECTION 16

Glossary of Gymnastics Terms[14]

Adolph: A front somersault with 3½ twists.

Aerial: A cartwheel (side aerial) or front walkover (front aerial) where the hands do not come in contact with the floor.

Amplitude: The amount of lift, repulsion, or extension of a particular skill.

Apparatus: A piece of equipment used in gymnastics training or competition.

Arabesque: A pose on one leg with the other leg extended behind the body.

Arch position: A curvature of the body in a reverse direction.

Assemble': A simple dance maneuver where the legs are brought together in the air to a landing with legs still together.

Attitude: The mental frame of reference displayed by a gymnast.

Back handspring: A move where a gymnast takes off from one or two feet, jumps backward onto the hands and pikes down to land on the feet; also known as a "flic-flac" or "flip-flop".

Back: A backward somersault.

Back-in, full-out: Two continuous backwards somersaults with a full twist performed during the second somersault.

Balance beam: A sixteen-foot beam, 4-inches wide and approximately 4-feet above the floor, used for routines involving leaps, turns and tumbling moves in women's artistic gymnastics.

Balance': A connection of three dance steps with a demi-plie' on the first step and releve' on the last two steps.

Balance: A static position like a scale or handstand position.

Barani: Similar to a forward somersault with a half-twist, only the twist occurs early in the somersault.

---

[14] This glossary created by combining terms from several sources: "Gymnastics: A Guide for Parents and Athletes," "Sequential Gymnastics II," Women's Junior Olympic Compulsory Exercises - 1997," and author's descriptions.

Basic Stand: A stand with the legs together and extended, torso erect, head neutral.

Beatboard / Reuter Board: The vault board used in the men's and women's vault at the Olympic level.

Bed: The area of a trampoline on which competitors bounce.

Body wave: A wave-like movement of the entire body passing through the hips, shoulders, arms and head.

Bridge: An arched position with the feet and hands flat on the floor and the abdomen up.

Cabriole': A leap where one leg is raised to the front and the other leg is brought up swiftly underneath and beats against it before the gymnast lands on the foot used for take-off.

Candlestick: A balance position high on the shoulders, with the hip angle open and body extended.

Cartwheel: A sideways / lateral kick to handstand then step down sideways with arms and legs extended.

Cast: From a front support (on uneven bars or horizontal bar), hands in overgrip, flexing at the hips (90 degrees) and immediately thrusting the legs backward and upward while maintaining the support position with extended arms.

Cat leap: A leap where a gymnast takes off from one foot, raising one knee and then the other.

Chaine' turn: A turn on the balls of the feet.

Chasse': A movement of the feet, either forwards or sideways which gives the impression of one foot chasing the other. (Often mispronounced as "Sa-shay.")

Clear Stride Support: On Uneven Bars - one leg on each side of bar (one leg forward, one leg backward). Hands support the body so that it remains off of the bar.

Clear: Movements in which only the hands (not the body) are in contact with the apparatus.

Composition: The structure of a gymnastics routine.

Compulsories: Pre-designed routines that contain specific movements required of all gymnasts.

Contraction: Forward, then retract the abdominal wall backward.

Counterswing: A backward swing on the bars.

Coupe': A term describing the position of the leg. The leg is bent with the toe pointed on or behind the ankle, depending on the position of the support leg (parallel or turned out).

Cross: A position on the men's rings where the arms are straight out sideways, supporting the body, which is held vertically.

Demi-plie': Position of the legs and feet used in preparation for jumps and turns and in landings. The knees are slightly flexed and turned out along with the feet.

Develope': The unfolding of a leg into an open position in the air.

Diagonal tumbling: Male and female gymnasts commonly place their difficult tumbling skills on the diagonal, which is tumbling from corner to corner across the middle of the floor rather than tumbling from corner to corner on the sides of the floor area.

Difficulty: A rating that measures the difficulty of specific moves and is factored into the total score after judges have scored the execution of the moves.

Dismount: The final skill performed in a routine that must be stuck on landing, that is to take no steps on completion and then salute to the judges.

Double stag ring leap: Similar to the double stag leap, but with the back arched so that the foot of the back leg is at or above head height.

Double stag: A split leap where both legs are bent in the front and the back.

Element: A single skill or dance movement that has been assigned a degree of difficulty and or value in a gymnastics routine.

Execution: The form, style, amplitude, timing and technique used to complete the skills included in a routine in their appropriate sequence.

Flank: A skill in which the body passes over a piece of equipment with the side of the body facing the apparatus.

Flexibility: Flexibility is the range of motion through which a body part, such as the shoulders or legs, can move without feeling pain, while maintaining strength and stability of the joint.

Flic-flac / Flip-flop: A move where a gymnast takes off from one or two feet, jumps backward onto the hands and lands on the feet; also known as a "flip-flop" or "back handspring".

Floor exercise: An event in men's and women's artistic gymnastics where a gymnast performs a series of exercises on an open 42' by 42' square of mats (with springs underneath) covered with carpet.

Flyaway: An Uneven Bar dismount performed from a long swing to finish with a salto.

Fouette: Push off one leg while kicking the other leg forward and upward executing a 180 degree turn, and land on the take-off leg. The other leg remains extended rearward.

Front Support: Any support position where the arms are straight and extended in front of the body.

Full-in, back-out: A double back ward's somersault with a full twist performed during the first somersault.

Giant: A swing through 360 degrees around the bar, with the body fully extended.

Glide: A forward swing on the low bar that finishes with the body extended.

Grand jete: A scissor-like movement from one leg to the other with legs outstretched in the air.

Grand plie: A position where the gymnast stands with legs fully bent.

Half-in, half-out: A double somersault with a half-twist on each somersault.

Handspring: (Front handspring) A common term for a gymnastics element where the gymnast kicks up to and through a handstand by punching out of the shoulders and driving the heels over to land in a stand. (Back handspring) From a stand the gymnast jumps backward to land in a handstand position from which he or he pikes down to a stand.

Handstand: Hands are flat on the floor, shoulder width apart, and the body completely extended and straight, legs together.

Headstand: Place the hands and forehead on the floor in a triangular shape (head in front of hands), and extend the hips and legs straight upward over the triangular base of support.

High bar: A bar standing approximately 9' high used in men's artistic gymnastics; also called the "horizontal bar".

Hitchkick: Push upward off one leg while swinging the other leg forward and upward, switching legs in the air, and landing on the other foot, in a demi-plie'.

Hop: Take off one foot to land on the same foot.

Hurdle: A long, low, and powerful skip step, which may be preceded by a run. The hurdle is a transition from a run or jump into a gymnastics skill.

Inverted: Any position in which the lower body is moved into a position above the upper body.

Inward turn: A turn in the direction of the supporting leg or arm; also known as a "reverse turn".

Jete': A graceful move where a gymnast springs from one foot to the other.

Jump: Moving from both feet to both feet.

Kip: A move from a hanging position below an apparatus to a support position above it, usually completed from a glide swing.

Landing Mat: A four to eight-inch mat filled with foam and ethyfoam to soften the landing when a gymnast dismounts the apparatus.

Layout: A straight or slightly arched position of the body.

Leap: Moving from one foot to the other foot showing flight.

Leg circle: A standard pommel-horse move where a gymnast keeps the legs together and swings them in a full circle around the horse, with each hand lifted in turn from the pommel to let the legs pass.

Lever: From a basic stand on one foot, the free leg is lifted behind with the arms stretched overhead, creating a straight line from the fingertips to toes. The hip joint acts as a fulcrum about which the arms and legs pivot as a unit. Lever positions should be seen when moving into or out of handstand skills.

Lunge: A lunge is a position in which one leg is flexed approximately 90 degrees, and the other leg is straight and extended. The body is stretched and upright over the flexed leg.

Mixed grip: One hand in overgrip and the other in undergrip.

Mount: The initial skill of a gymnastics routine.

Opposition: A position of the arms whereby one arm is placed in a forward-middle position and the opposite arm in side-middle.

Optionals: Routines created by the gymnast which portray their best skills and personality.

Overgrip: Grasping the bar with the thumbs pointing towards each other.

Panel Mats: Basic mats which are constructed of a single layer of resilient foam, ranging in thickness from one to two inches, that can be folded into panels approximately two feet wide.

Parallel bars: An apparatus consisting of two wood-laminated fiberglass rails on uprights, adjustable in height and used for swinging, vaulting and balancing exercises in men's artistic gymnastics.

Parallette: A training apparatus that is a smaller version of the parallel bars used on a matted area for training purposes.

Passe': A position of the leg whereby one leg is bent with the toe pointed against the inside of the knee of the support leg. (May be performed with the knee pointed forward or sideward)

Pike: A position where the body is bent forward at the hips to 90 degrees or more while the legs are kept straight, with the thighs close to the upper body.

Pirouette: To turn on one foot around the body's longitudinal axis, as defined by the spine, in dance elements. Also descriptive of a move when the body is in a handstand position and the hands are used to rotate the body around it's longitudinal axis.

Pivot: A sharp 1/2 turn around a single point of support, like one hand or a turn on the ball of the foot.

Plane: An imaginary surface where moves are performed, i.e., lateral, frontal, horizontal or diagonal.

Plie': A position with the knees bent and the back straight.

Pommel horse: A men's event similar to the vault horse but with two wooden pommels about which circling movements of the legs are performed.

Presentation: (present) - a movement of the arms whereby the arm(s) open from forward-middle to a side-middle position.

Prone: Lying face down with the body straight.

Randolph/ Randy: A front somersault with 2½ twists; also known as a "Randy".

Rear Support: Any support position where the arms are straight and extended behind the body.

Rear: A descriptive term indicating that the body passes over or around an apparatus with the back of the body leading or facing the apparatus.

Rebound: A quick jump using very little flexion of the hips, knees, or ankles.

Release: To leave the bar to perform a move before grasping it again.

Releve': A swift rise or lift onto the ball of the foot.

Reverse turn: A turn in the direction of the supporting leg; also known as an "inward turn".

Rhythm: The speed or tempo at which a skill/dance step is performed.

Ring leap: A leap where the legs are in a splits position, with the front leg straight and the back leg bent, while the back, head and arms are arched backward, forming a "ring" shape.

Rings: Two parallel rings, suspended from a cable and straps and held, one in each hand, for a series of exercises in men's artistic gymnastics particularly requiring stillness of the body; also called the "still rings".

Round-off: A round-off is a dynamic turning movement. Step forward and push off one leg while swinging the legs upward in a fast cartwheel type motion. As the body becomes inverted, execute a 90-degree turn, push off the hand, the legs are brought together just before landing facing the direction from which the performer started.

Routine: A combination of gymnastic, acrobatic, and dance elements displaying a full range of skills on one apparatus.

Rudolph / Rudy: A front somersault with 1½ twists; also known as a "Rudy".

Scale: A balance on one leg, with the other leg raised backward, sideward or forward and the upper body lowered slightly.

Scissor kick: A jump from one foot to the other with legs straightened as they swing forward, simulating the motion of scissors.

Scissors: A standard pommel-horse skill where the legs straddle the horse as they swing around it and the hands are lifted in turn to let the leg pass.

Sequence: Two or more positions or skills, which are performed together creating a different skill or activity.

Side splits: A position where a gymnast sits on the floor with the legs at full horizontal extension on opposite sides of the body, forming a 180-degree split.

Sissone: Stepping forward on one foot, bringing the other foot forward to a position behind the first, jump and separate the legs to a split position, and land on the first leg.

Skill: A specific move that competitors are required to perform.

SLP: Safety Landing Position. When landing from a gymnastics skill the athlete lands with knees bent, lower back rounded, and arms up next to the ears.

Snap: A very quick movement of the body, usually form a 3/4 handstand position, moving the feet to the ground bringing the body to a near upright position.

Somersault: A flip or rollover in the air where a gymnast rotates around the axis of the hips.

Split leap: A forward leap from one foot, landing on the opposite foot and assuming a split position in mid-air.

Splits: A position where one leg is extended forward and the other backward, at right angles to the body.

Spot: To spot is to physically guide and/or assist a gymnast while performing a skill. Coaches spot for safety and when they are teaching new skills.

Spotters: Usually the coach or an individual whose job it is to protect competitors from injury should they fall.

Springboard / Vault Board: The device used to launch a gymnast into the air over a vault horse. Usually has 3 to 6 springs mounted between two boards, the top board being covered with carpet.

Squared hips: A position of the body whereby both hips are flat and facing forward.

Squat: Support on the balls of the feet with the knees and hips flexed so that the seat is near, but not touching the floor with the heels and torso erect.

Stag leap: A leap where the front leg is bent at the knee and the other leg extends straight back behind the body.

Stick: A gymnast "sticks" a landing when he/he executes a landing with correct technique and no movement of the feet.

Straddle: A position in which the legs are straight and extended sideward.

Straight Stand: Standing with the heels together at a position of attention.

Stretch Position: Standing straight with the arms extended above your head.

Stride support: A position on the bars whereby the weight is balanced on the hands with one leg on each side of the bar.(one leg forward, one leg backward)

Supine (Layout Position): Lying flat on the back with the body straight, arms extended above the head.

Tkatchev: Named after Russian gymnast Alexander Tkatchev, a move from a backward giant to a backward straddle release over the bar.

Tour jete': Push off one leg while kicking the other leg forward and upward executing a 180 degree turn, switch the legs in the air, and land on the first leg. The take-off leg is extended rearward.

Tripod: Place the hands and forehead on the floor in a triangular shape (head in front of hands), and extend the hips above the triangular base. The body is piked with the knees bent, resting on the elbows.

Tuck: A position where the knees and hips are bent and drawn into the chest.

Turn: A rotation on the body's axis supported by one or both feet.

Twist: A move in acrobatic skills where a gymnast rotates around the body's longitudinal axis, defined by the spine.

Undergrip: Grasping the bar with both thumbs facing out, away from each other.

Uneven bars: An apparatus in women's artistic gymnastics with a top bar almost 10 feet above the floor and a lower bar 4 1/2' high, used for a continuous series of grip changes, releases, new grasps and other complex moves.

Vault: A solid apparatus similar to the pommel horse, but lacking handles, and used in men's and women's artistic gymnastics for a variety of handsprings from a running approach.

V-sit: A position where the legs are raised off the floor close together and the body is supported by the hands to form a "V" shape.

Walkover: A gymnast kicks up from a standing position through a handstand position to a standing position while "walking" through the air with the feet.

Waltz Step: Three consecutive steps, demi-plie' through 4th position on the first step and releve' on the next two steps.

Wedge: A developmental mat filled with soft, shock absorbent foam. Its distinct shape is a sloping triangle with various heights and widths.

Wedgie: When a gymnasts leotard or shorts are riding up their rear.

Yurchenko vault: Named after Soviet gymnast Natalia Yurchenko, a vault that begins with a round-off entry onto the vault board and continues with a back handspring onto the horse and a back 1½ somersault off.

SECTION 17: MISCELLANEOUS AND FORMS

Lesson Plans / Skill Evaluation / Record Keeping

As you may have noted throughout this training system, great emphasis has been placed on Safety and to a similar degree you have been notified about legal concerns that could involve you as the instructor should a child get injured while in your care.

Unfortunately, as we stated at the outset in the Special Notice at the beginning of the manual accident and injury could happen anywhere – even with the best of training and precautions. Please do not assume because you have done everything correctly or because you enjoy a certain friendship with the parents of an injured child that you may not have to face any legal action. The realities of emergency care, hospital costs, and rehabilitation may financially force the parents of an injured gymnast to sue.

In addition, don't assume that the "business" insurance will cover all costs. Using a process called "contributory negligence" the legal system may find you are partly at fault for the child's injury. For sake of argument, let's say the legal system declares you contributed 10% of the reason the child got injured. The jury awards one million dollars in damages. Do you have one hundred thousand dollars to payoff the jury award?

The thought is scary and I should tell you that this is not unique to the sport of gymnastics; it is true of any and all activities where you are in a position of authority over anyone – even as a homeowner allowing neighborhood kids to play in your yard. The solution to this potential problem is preparation and follow through.

Preparation:
11. Supervise the activity closely.
12. Properly plan the activity.
13. Provide proper instruction.
14. Provide a safe physical environment.
15. Provide adequate and proper equipment.
16. Warn of inherent risks.
17. Provide appropriate emergency assistance.
18. Keep informed.
19. Know your students.
20. Keep adequate records.

Follow Through:
1. Review and assess your ability to follow the "10 Preparation Guidelines" daily.
2. Use an effective Lesson Planning system.
3. Track the results of your lesson plans, and then modify the lessons based on the results.
4. Keep records of all lesson plans and results tracking for future reference.

How good is your memory?

It had better be excellent in the extreme if you don't do lesson plans or keep records of skill achievement in class because I can guarantee you that will be one of the things any lawyer asks you if you become involved in any litigation arising from a child who gets injured while in your care.

Some things you should keep in mind are that the parents of an injured child may sue directly, but did you know that the child himself, upon reaching eighteen years of age, has a few years within which to initiate a law suit regarding an injury received while a child? Can you specifically remember several years into the past what you were teaching in any particular class?

Lesson Plans

Don't take any chances; keep a set of lesson plans for every class you teach. To make that task manageable we have provided you with a series of lesson planning charts by event. For instance, the skills in Level 1 Vault are all listed down the left side of the chart. To the right of each skill are eight blanks spaces which represent the next eight classes you are about to teach at this level. Using the key provided at the bottom of the chart: **Key = Introductory, R = Review, M = Maintenance, C = Circuit Element, T = Test,** you can determine the skills you want to work.

At the top of the chart, in the space provided, record the date of the class. In the empty blocks below, record which skills you plan to work that day. If you have never worked the skill before you would place an "I" for Introductory. Similarly, if you have worked it before but want to review it you would place an "R." If you want to make it part of a circuit with some other skills, you place a "C" in the squares of those skills that make up your circuit. When you plan to Test or evaluate an element, place a "T" in that square.

The advantage to this system is that each week you can easily see what you worked the week before. In fact, if a substitute ever had to take over your class he/he would immediately have a record of what you have been training.

Skill Evaluation Form

The Skill Evaluation Form looks almost identical to the Lesson Plan Form except instead of dates across the top you will list the class member's names. Every time you put a **"T"** on the Lesson Plan Form you will record the results of that test on the Skill Evaluation Form using the following key: **/ = Fair, X = Good, ★ = Excellent.** If the gymnast is incapable of performing the skill the instructor will leave the square blank. If the gymnast makes the skill but the form is sloppy you will make a slash mark across the square; if the gymnast makes the skill and it looks good you will make an X across the square; and, if he does the skill with excellent form you place a star in the square.

The beauty of this system is that you can use the Skill Evaluation Form to help you determine the Lesson Plans for the next week's class. Wherever you see empty squares or squares with slashes you know these are skills that need to be worked. You can also see gymnast's who need to move to the next level or who need to stay for another session at this level.

Special Note:

Like the stars up in the night sky, the stars awarded in this system should be equally hard to reach. In today's society, there seems to be a trend toward equalization of award regardless of effort applied. Fortunately, gymnastics is a sport where only the individual's effort will get them the skill they desire. If you as an instructor raise a child to their highest level of incompetence by awarding stars they really have not earned, the child will more than likely soon quit out of frustration as those around his who truly made the grade continue to progress. In addition, you will defeat the purpose of this system, which is to accurately track individual and class progress to provide feedback for future lesson plans.

In addition, if another coach substitutes for you in a class and your records of the class ability are overstated, you could be putting those children into a situation they are not prepared for and could be the cause of potential injury. Be honest, be accurate, and be polite with belligerent parents who want their child to be rewarded for lack of skill – your response should focus on one concern – the child's safety.

Recordkeeping

Every time you complete one of these forms you should make a copy for your personal files and make sure that the original is on file at the gym. Should a child get hurt during class, no matter how minor, make a note on the back of your lesson plan and be sure to inform the parents. Any injury requiring a rest from activity, or if you are in the least suspicious about its severity, requires an accident report form be filled out. Again, keep a copy for your personal file and file the original with the club.

Your ability to demonstrate complete and accurate lesson plans, evaluations, and accident report forms, along with your continued educational development as a coach will go a long way in convincing the legal system that you handled yourself in a reasonable and prudent fashion as a professional gymnastics instructor.

Date of Class →									
Fl. Exercise/ Tumbling – Level 1 Lesson Plan Form ↓ **Skill to Train**									
1. Splits (right) 120 -140									
2. Splits (left) 120 -140									
3. Straddle split – 120									
4. Bridge									
5. Shoulder stand									
6. Swedish Fall									
7. Knee scale									
8. Tripod									
9. Tucked headstand									
10. Relevé Stand									
11. Two foot releve` ½ turn									
12. Scale (low back leg)									
13. Forward Passé`									
14. Squat ½ turn									
15. Handstand on the wall									
16. Prone fall from knees									
17. Cast hips up from knees									
18. Front to rear support									
19. Log rolls									
20. Ballet positions									
21. Front attitude position									
22. Assemble`									
23. Stretch jump (punch jumps)									
24. V-sit									
25. Tip up (two point balance)									
26. Tripod tuck hdstand									
27. Tuck forward roll down incline									
28. Tuck fwd roll to squat stand									
29. Tuck fwd roll to straddle sit									
30. Tuck fwd roll straddle stand									
31. Lead up to a cartwheel									
32. Cartwheel									
33. Back roll str std dwn incline									
34. Tuck back roll sit on heels									
35. Tuck back roll feet to feet									

Key: I = Introductory, R = Review, M = Maintenance, C = Circuit Element, T = Test

Name of Gymnast →								
Fl. Exercise/Tumbling – Level 1 Class Evaluation Form ↓ Skill to Evaluate								
1. Splits (right) 120 -140								
2. Splits (left) 120 -140								
3. Straddle split – 120								
4. Bridge								
5. Shoulder stand								
6. Swedish Fall								
7. Knee scale								
8. Tripod								
9. Tucked headstand								
10. Relevé Stand								
11. Two foot releve` ½ turn								
12. Scale (low back leg)								
13. Forward Passé`								
14. Squat ½ turn								
15. Handstand on the wall								
16. Prone fall from knees								
17. Cast hips up from knees								
18. Front to rear support								
19. Log rolls								
20. Ballet positions								
21. Front attitude position								
22. Assemble`								
23. Stretch jump (punch jumps)								
24. V-sit								
25. Tip up (two point balance)								
26. Tripod tuck hdstand								
27. Tuck forward roll down incline								
28. Tuck fwd roll to squat stand								
29. Tuck fwd roll to straddle sit								
30. Tuck fwd roll straddle stand								
31. Lead up to a cartwheel								
32. Cartwheel								
33. Back roll str std dwn incline								
34. Tuck back roll sit on heels								
35. Tuck back roll feet to feet								

Key: / = Fair, X = Good, ★ = Excellent

Date of Class →								
Vault – Level 1 Lesson Plan Form ↓ Skill to Train								
1. Safety Landing Position								
2. Arm & Leg Synch– March								
3. Skipping								
4. Step hurdle – no board.								
5. Step hurdle bkwd arm circle								
6. Run – no board								
7. Stretch jump over objects								
8. Punch jumps board w/spot								
9. Jump from board (no run)								
10. Jump to board w/arm cir, rbd.								
11. Pnch jmps on board w/o hands								
12. R/H/P bd, str jmp- safety land.								
13. R/H/P board, tuck jump								
straddle, pike, ½ turn, 1/1 turn.								
15. Jump – jump – tuck jump								
16. Jump – jump – straddle jump								
17. Jump – jump – pike jump								
18. Squat Thrusts								
19. Bounces to squat on, jump off								
20. Squat on, jump off (from walk)								
21. Squat on, jump off (from run)								
22. Squat Vault								
23. Double jump – jump ½ turn								
24. Triple jump – forward roll								
25. Traveling jumps								

Key = Introductory, R = Review, M = Maintenance, C = Circuit Element, T = Test

Name of Gymnast→								
Vault – Level 1 **Skill Evaluation Form** ↓ **Skill to Evaluate**								
1. Safety Landing Position								
2. Arm & Leg Synch– March								
3. Skipping								
4. Step hurdle – no board.								
5. Step hurdle bkwd arm circle								
6. Run – no board								
7. Stretch jump over objects								
8. Punch jumps board w/spot								
9. Jump from board (no run)								
10. Jump to board w/arm cir, rbd.								
11. Pnch jmps on board w/o hands								
12. R/H/P bd, str jmp- safety land.								
13. R/H/P board, tuck jump								
straddle, pike, ½ turn, 1/1 turn.								
15. Jump – jump – tuck jump								
16. Jump – jump – straddle jump								
17. Jump – jump – pike jump								
18. Squat Thrusts								
19. Bounces to squat on, jump off								
20. Squat on, jump off (from walk)								
21. Squat on, jump off (from run)								
22. Squat Vault								
23. Double jump – jump ½ turn								
24. Triple jump – forward roll								
25. Traveling jumps								

Key: **/** = Fair, **X** = Good, **★**= Excellent

Date of class → **High Bar – Level 1 Lesson Plan Form** ↓ Skill to Train									
1. Single Bar Grips									
2. Front support – low bar									
3. Rear support – low bar									
4. Climb to perch stand									
5. Skin the cat / long hang position									
6. Pike inverted hang									
7. Straight body inverted hang									
8. Single knee hang									
9. Glide hang									
10. Tuck inverted hang									
11. Grip walks									
12. Long Hang Swings									
13. Fwd roll low bar to stand									
14. 3 cast preparations									
15. Cast Off - Come Back to Bar									
16. Cast off low bar to stand									
17. Hock swing– Hands on low bar									
18. Glide Swing – Low Bar									
19. Perch sole hang dismount.									
20. Jump sole hang dsmt – straddle									
21. Single knee swing up									
22. Stride support low bar									
23. Hip Pullover Low Bar									
24. Sm cast back hip cir tuck									
25. Sm cast back hip cir pike									
26. Sm cast back hip cir stretched									

Key: I = Introductory, R = Review, M = Maintenance, C = Circuit Element, T = Test

Name of Gymnast →									
High Bars – Level 1 Skill Evaluation ↓ Skill to Evaluate									
1. Single Bar Grips									
2. Front support – low bar									
3. Rear support – low bar									
4. Climb to perch stand									
5. Skin the cat / long hang pos									
6. Pike inverted hang									
7. Straight body inverted hang									
8. Single knee hang									
9. Glide hang									
10. Tuck inverted hang									
11. Grip walks									
12. Long Hang Swings									
13. Fwd roll low bar to stand									
14. 3 cast preparations									
15. Cast Off - Come Back to Bar									
16. Cast off low bar to stand									
17. Hock swing– low bar									
18. Glide Swing – Low Bar									
19. Perch sole hang dismount.									
20. Jump str sole hang dsmt									
21. Single knee swing up									
22. Stride support low bar									
23. Hip Pullover Low Bar									
24. Sm cast back hip cir tuck									
25. Sm cast back hip cir pike									
26. Sm cast back hip cir stretched									

Key: / = Fair, X = Good, ★ = Excellent

Date of Class → **Pommels – Level 1 Lesson Plan Form** ↓ Skill to Train								
1. Front Support (Floor)								
2. Rear Support (Floor)								
3. Support on One Arm (Floor)								
4. Mushroom Front Support								
5. Mushroom Rear Support								
6. Mushroom Support 1 Arm								
7. Mushroom Support other Arm								
8. Walk around the mushroom								
9. Hop around mshrm w/ 360								
10. ¾ Hop around mshrm 270								
11. Front Support on P H								
12. Rear Support on PH								
13. Front Straddle Swings								
14. Rear Straddle Swings								
15. Front Straddle Swings lift arm								
16. Rear Straddle Swings lift arm								
17. Walk over different objects.								
18. Single Leg Cut (Right Leg)								
19. Single Leg Cut (Left Leg)								
20. Frwd. leg cut rt then leg cut left								
21. Bckwd leg cut rt then leg cut left								
* Stride Support								

Gymnast Name → **Pommels – Level 1 Evaluation Form** Skill to Evaluate								
1. Front Support (Floor)								
2. Rear Support (Floor)								
3. Support on One Arm (Floor)								
4. Mushroom Front Support								
5. Mushroom Rear Support								
6. Mushroom Support 1 Arm								
7. Mushroom Support other Arm								
8. Walk around the mushroom								
9. Hop around mshrm w/ 360								
10. ¾ Hop around mshrm 270								
11. Front Support on P H								
12. Rear Support on PH								
13. Front Straddle Swings								
14. Rear Straddle Swings								
15. Front Straddle Swings lift arm								
16. Rear Straddle Swings lift arm								
17. Walk over different objects.								
18. Single Leg Cut (Right Leg)								
19. Single Leg Cut (Left Leg)								
20. Frwd. leg cut rt then leg cut left								
21. Bckwd leg cut rt then leg cut left								
* Stride Support								

Key: / = Fair, X = Good, ★ = Excellent

Date of Class →								
Rings – Level 1 Lesson Plan Form ↓ Skill to Train								
1. Straight Body Hang (with control)								
2. .Hang in Tuck (with control)								
3. Hang in L Hold (with control)								
4. Inverted Pike Hold								
5. Inverted Hang (straight body)								
6. Skin-the-cat								
7. Forward Swing								
8. Backward Swing								
9. Swing to Inverted Hang								
10. Swing to Inverted Hang to pike								
11. Swing to Inv Hang, pike, skin cat								
12. Inlocate and dislocate								
Strength Skills								
1. Chin Up on Rings and Hold 10 sec								
2. Hang in Tuck Position Hold 10 sec								
3. Hang in L Position Hold for 10 sec								
4. Hang in Straddle w/ legs straight								
5. Pull feet to rings and hold								

Key: I = Introductory, R = Review, M = Maintenance, C = Circuit Element, T = Test

Name of Gymnast →								
Rings – Level 1 **Class Evaluation Form** ↓ Skill to Evaluate								
1. Straight Body Hang (with control)								
2. .Hang in Tuck (with control)								
3. Hang in L Hold (with control)								
4. Inverted Pike Hold								
5. Inverted Hang (straight body)								
6. Skin-the-cat								
7. Forward Swing								
8. Backward Swing								
9. Swing to Inverted Hang								
10. Swing to Inverted Hang to pike								
11. Swing to Inv Hang, pike, skin cat								
12. Inlocate and dislocate								
Strength Skills								
1. Chin Up on Rings and Hold 10 sec								
2. Hang in Tuck Position Hold 10 sec								
3. Hang in L Position Hold for 10 sec								
4. Hang in Straddle w/ legs straight								
5. Pull feet to rings and hold								

Key: / = Fair, X = Good, ★= Excellent

Date of Class → **Parallel Bars – Level 1 Lesson Plan Form** ↓ Skill to Train									
1. Straight Arm Support									
2. Arm Support in Tuck									
3. Arm Support in L									
4. From Support on FL w/ form									
5. Rear Support on Fl w/. form									
6. Straight Arm Support Swings									
7. Support Swings into Straddle									
7. Traveling Straddle Support swings									
8. Rear Dismount from Swing									
Strength Moves for P Bars									
1. Above Supports from arm pits									
2. Hang in Tuck Position Hold 10 sec									
3. Hang in L Position Hold for 10 sec									
4. Hang in Straddle w/ legs straight									

Key: I = Introductory, R = Review, M = Maintenance, C = Circuit Element, T = Test

Name of Gymnast →								
Parallel Bars – Level 1 Class Evaluation Form ↓ Skill to Evaluate								
1. Straight Arm Support								
2. Straight Arm Support in Tuck								
3. Straight Arm Support in L								
4. From Support on FL w/ form								
5. Rear Support on Fl w/. form								
6. Straight Arm Support Swings								
7. Support Swings into Straddle								
7. Traveling Straddle Support swings								
8. Rear Dismount from Swing								
Strength Moves for P Bars								
1. Above supports from arm pits								
2. Hang in Tuck Position Hold 10 sec								
3. Hang in L Position Hold for 10 sec								
4. Hang in Straddle w/ legs straight								

Key: / = Fair, X = Good, ★ = Excellent

Date of Class →									
Trampoline – Level 1 Lesson Plan Form ↓ Skill to Train									
1. Climb on and off safely									
2. 10 Bounces with control									
3. Bounce and stop with control									
4. Tuck jump									
5. Straddle jump									
6. Tuck jump, strdl jump – stop									
7. Star jump									
8. Pike jump									
9. Jump ½ & 1/1 turn									
10. Seat drop to stand									
11. Seat drop ½ turn to stand.									
12. Tuck jump extend to seat drop extend to straddle, return to stand									

Date of Class →									
Strength – Level 1 Lesson Plan Form ↓ Skill to Train									
1. 20 sit-ups (up to 20)									
2. 6 push-ups									
3. 6 arch-ups									
4. Pike stretch – fingertips									
5. Tuck L – 2 seconds									
6. Punch jumps – 45 sec.									
7. 5 squat jumps									
8. 1 pull up									
9. 1 leg lift – bars									
10. Leg lifts – floor F/S/B									
11. Run – 1 minute									
12. 5 inlocate-dislocates									

Key: I = Introductory, R = Review, M = Maintenance, C = Circuit Element, T = Test

Name of Gymnast→ Trampoline – Level 1 Skill Evaluation Form ↓ Skill to Evaluate								
1. Climb on and off safely								
2. 10 Bounces with control								
3. Bounce and stop with control								
4. Tuck jump								
5. Straddle jump								
6. Tuck jump, strdl jump – stop								
7. Star jump								
8. Pike jump								
9. Jump ½ & 1/1 turn								
10. Seat drop to stand								
11. Seat drop ½ turn to stand.								
12. Tuck jump extend to seat drop extend to straddle, return to stand								

Key: / = Fair, X = Good, ★ = Excellent

Name of Gymnast → Strength – Level 1 Skill Evaluation Form ↓ Skill to Evaluate								
1. 20 sit-ups (up to 20)								
2. 6 push-ups								
3. 6 arch-ups								
4. Pike stretch – fingertips								
5. Tuck L – 2 seconds								
6. Punch jumps – 45 sec.								
7. 5 squat jumps								
8. 1 pull up								
9. 1 leg lift – bars								
10. Leg lifts – floor F/S/B								
11. Run – 1 minute								
12. 5 inlocate-dislocates								

(Strength score by numbers completed)

ACCIDENT REPORT FORM
(To be filled out by the instructor supervising the gymnastics class / workout)

Today's Date:_____ Time:_____am / pm (circle one)

Gymnast's Name:_____Age:_____

Last name of parent if different from gymnast:_____

Address:_____

City:_____State:_____Zip:_____

Home Phone: _____Work Phone:_____

Emergency Contact:_____Ph#_____

Name of First-Aider / Responder:_____

Phone:_____Position:_____

Facility Name: (where accident occurred)_____

Name of gymnastics apparatus:_____

Skill being attempted:_____

Anatomical area involved:_____

Cause of injury:_____

Extent of injury:_____

_____

_____

First Aid administered:_____

_____

Referral action: (parent, hospital, 911)_____

Parent notified? (circle one)   Yes / No   Time:_____am / pm (circle one)

Witness (es) names & phone numbers:_____

_____

Signature of First Aider / Responder:_____

EMERGENCY ACTION PLAN

1. Make sure all emergency numbers are posted by each phone in the gym and a copy is pasted onto the First Aid kit. Make sure everyone knows where the nearest phone is located, especially if you are outside your normal facility. (See copy of *Emergency Call Card.*)

2. Make sure another athlete, coach, or parent is able to get to that phone. Will they need keys? Do the phones have special dialing codes? Do they need change for the phone?

3. If there is a suspected head or neck injury, or if you are unsure of the extent of injury - **DO NOT MOVE THE ATHLETE!** Wait for properly trained medical assistance.

4. If an athletic trainer is not available, apply proper First Aid until trained medical help arrives.

5. Never leave an injured athlete alone. Always send someone else to call for help. You should stay to reassure the athlete and monitor vital signs.

6. Designate someone to keep control of the crowd, spectators, or other athletes involved. Re-direct the practice or demonstration if possible. Send remaining athletes to workout in a separate area or have the demonstration moved to an area away from the injured athlete. Remember, chaos causes panic. Panic can often cause a minor injury to instantly become a serious one.

7. Send someone to wait for the ambulance by the nearest road so that he / he can direct the help immediately to the injured athlete. **Note:** Are all gates and doors unlocked so the ambulance can get through?

8. In most cases, parents are not trained for emergency situations and their presence leads to panic in the injured athlete. Parents are advised to stay back until called upon by the coaches or emergency medical personnel.

9. Have an adult (coach or parent) ride with the injured athlete in the ambulance. Make sure they take the *Emergency Information and Consent Card* with them.

10. If the athletes parents are not present, make sure they are notified as soon as possible and have them meet the athlete at the hospital.

11. Document and date the injury and all subsequent events relating to the accident. Keep one copy for yourself and turn in a copy to your club owner or program director for proper filing. Accident reports should be kept for a minimum of three years.

INFORMATION FOR EMERGENCY CALLS:

(Be prepared to give this information to the 911 / EMS dispatcher)

1. Facility Name: _____

2. Street Address: _____

3. City / Town: _____

4. Directions (cross streets, landmarks, etc.) _____

_____

_____

5. Phone # from which this call is made:_____

6. Tell the dispatcher what your name is.

7. Tell the dispatcher about the injury or accident that occurred.

8. How many persons were injured? Tell dispatcher.

9. Condition of victims. Tell dispatcher.

10. Help (first aid) being given. Tell dispatcher.

NOTE: Do not hang up the phone until the EMS dispatcher (911 operator) tells you to hang up.

Report to first aider / responder that help is on the way.

Obtain *"Emergency Consent Form"* for medical treatment for the gymnast in question for transport to the hospital with paramedics.

Send a responsible person to flag down the ambulance from the road nearest your facility (preferably an adult), and make sure all gates and access ways are unlocked.

Fill out *"Accident Report Form"* immediately.

References:

Babbitt, Diane H. and Werner Haas. Gymnastic apparatus exercises for girls. New York: Ronald Press, c 1964.

Bowers, Carolyn O., editor. Selected gymnastics articles. Washington : AAHPR, c 1971.

Buchholtz, Stan. Balancing & Sport Acrobatics. New York: Arco Publishing, c1978.

Feeney, Rik. Gymnastics: A Guide for Parents and Athletes. Indianapolis: Masters Press, c1992.

Feeney, Rik. Gymnastics: A Guide for Parents and Athletes.(electronic version @ Booklocker.com) Albemarle, NC: Richardson Publishing, c2000.

Feeney, Rik. Safety Basics Every Gymnastics Instructor Should Know. Apopka, FL: Richardson Publishing, c1996.

Feeney, Rik. How to Create Exciting Lesson Plans. Apopka, FL: Richardson Publishing, c1996.

Feeney, Rik. GymText. Albemarle, NC: Richardson Publishing, c1998.

Fukushima, Sho and Wrio Russell. Men's gymnastics. Boston: Faber & Faber, c 1980.

George, Gerald S. Biomechanics of women's gymnastics. Englewood Cliffs, N.J.: Prentice-Hall, c 1980.

Griswold, Larry and Glenn Wilson. Trampoline Tumbling Today. 1948, 1962. New York: A. S. Barnes, c1970.

Guinness, Alma E. (editor). ABC's of the Human Body. New York: Reader's Digest, c1987.

Horne, Virginia Lee. Stunts and Tumbling for Girls. New York: Ronald Press, c1943.

Johnson, Barry L. and Mary J. Garcia. Gymnastics for the Beginner. New York: Harper & Row, c1976.

Mosston, Musska. Developmental Movement. Columbus: Merrill Books, c 1965.

Murray, Mimi. Women's Gymnastics: Coach, Participant, Spectator. Boston: Allyn and Bacon, c1979.

Musker, Frank F., Donald R. Casady and Leslie W. Irwin. A guide to gymnastics. New York: Macmillan, c 1968.

Poole, Robert M. (editor). The Incredible Machine. Washington: National Geographic Society, c1986.

Sands, Bill and Mike Conklin. Everybody's Gymnastics Book. New York: Scribner's, c1984.

Sands, Bill. Coaching Women's Gymnastics. Champaign, IL: Human Kinetics, 1984.

Spackman, Jr, Robert R. Conditioning for gymnastics : pre-season, regular season, and off season. Springfield, IL: C. C. Thomas, c 1970.

Tanner, J. M. Fetus into Man: Physical Growth from Conception to Maturity. Cambridge, MA: Harvard University Press, c1978.

Wachtel, Erna and Newton C. Loken. Girls' Gymnastics. New York: Sterling, c1977.

Whitlock, Steve (editor). USA Gymnastics Safety Handbook. Indianapolis: USAG Publications, 1998.

Wiley, Jack. Acrobatics Book. Mountain View, CA: World Publications, c1978.

USA NATIONAL COACHING CERTIFICATION PROGRAM

USA Coaches Certification, Inc. is a web-based training course learning program for gymnastics coaches. Courses completed are Girl's Levels 1, Level 2, Level 3 for the Recreational Class Instructor, Girl's Level 4, Level 5 and Level 6 for the Compulsory Coach, GYMCERT's "Safety Basics" and Boys Level 1 Coaches Manual. This is the first manual for Boys, Level 1. USA Coaches Certification Inc. believes that the certification of gymnastics coaches will produce the following favorable outcomes:

1. **Provide a better and safer environment for gymnastics athletes.**
2. **Raise the standard of gymnastic coaches by aiding them to act in a proactive way by demonstrating their Risk Management procedures by taking the GYMCERT's courses.**
3. **Provide accountability of gymnastic coaches and gyms.**
4. **Lower the risk for insurance companies thus lowering the liability insurance rates for gym owners.**
5. **Cost savings for coaches and gym owners.**

By providing the automated gymnastics course via web-based training, coaches can obtain course materials, instruction, and may take the exams at their convenience. This saves everyone time and money that would have been spent taking time away from the gym, traveling to a seminar site, renting the venue, printing course materials, and hiring seminar leaders. More people will have access to the information as long as they have computer access with Internet connection. If the individual coach or their gym doesn't have this technology, every library has this technology available. Please view our web site at www.gymcert.com or contact us to order additional GYMCERT manuals and GYMCERT Safety Posters for your gym. GYMCERT'S "Safety Basics" is a MUST for your gymnastics library!

DATE DUE

			PRINTED IN U.S.A.

CPSIA information can be obtained
at www.ICGtesting.com
Printed in the USA
FFOW04n0937010518
46411775-48214FF

9 780974 549279